MW00653719

WHAT WE LEARNED FROM FOSTERING DOGS

One Family's Journal of

Pee, Poop, Heartache, and Unconditional Love

WHAT WE LEARNED FROM FOSTERING DOGS

One Family's Journal of

Pee, Poop, Heartache, and Unconditional Love

Rusty Williams

The Barefoot Ministries

WHAT WE LEARNED FROM FOSTERING DOGS

One Family's Journal of Pee, Poop, Heartache, and Unconditional Love

Copyright © 2022 by Rusty Williams.

All rights reserved. Printed in the United States of America. No part of this publication may be reproduced, distributed, or transmitted in any form or by any means, including photocopying, recording, or other electronic or mechanical methods, without the prior written permission of the publisher, except in the case of brief quotations embodied in critical reviews and certain other noncommercial uses permitted by copyright law.

ISBN: 978-1-7361579-5-4

First printing edition 2022

Published by The Barefoot Ministries
149 Sitting Bull Trail
Medford Lakes, NJ 08055

www.thebarefootministries.org

All scripture quotations and Bible references are from the New Revised Standard Version Bible, copyright ©1989, Division of Christian Education of the National Council of the Churches of Christ in the United States of America. Used by permission. All rights reserved.

This manuscript was previously published in 2015 under a contract with a publishing company that is no longer in business and has entered a plea agreement with the Oklahoma State Attorney General. It is being published in accordance with that plea agreement that released all rights of the manuscript and book back to its author. The author holds all rights to this book.

Lord, make me an instrument of your peace.

Where there is hatred, let me sow love.

Where there is injury, pardon.

Where there is doubt, faith.

Where there is despair, hope.

Where there is darkness, light.

Where there is sadness, joy.

O Divine Master,

grant that I may not so much seek to be consoled, as to console;

to be understood, as to understand;

to be loved, as to love.

For it is in giving that we receive.

It is in pardoning that we are pardoned,

and it is in dying that we are born to Eternal Life.

Amen.

—Prayer of Saint Francis

This book is dedicated to everyone involved with animal rescue organizations worldwide and in memory of all the pets that are waiting for us on the other side of the Rainbow Bridge.

In honor of everyone fighting an orphan disease.

For Matt and Corey.

To Elissa.

Foreword

.

Some books are meant to be read by lots and lots of people. Rusty Williams' book is one of them. It's a book you'll immediately want to share with everyone you care about. Like a good movie, *What We Learned From Fostering Dogs* will make you laugh, and it will make you cry. It will always keep you entertained. Most importantly, it will inspire you.

Now let me get one thing straight. This is a book about dogs and the amazing people who foster them. But it's more than that. Let me tell you why.

Each chapter comes with its own tale about a dog—and in some very funny instances, more than one dog—that Rusty and his wife, Elissa, cared for until the foster care community could arrange an adoption. The stories are laugh-out-loud funny, suspenseful, and heartwarming. If you're a dog lover, or, I'll go even further, if you have ever cared for an animal, you're going to love this book. There are a lot of people already on my list who are going to get *What We Learned From Fostering Dogs* for the holidays.

But here's what I want to get right. Here's how this book is much more than just about foster dogs. Rusty is a truly wise man and a master storyteller, and like the great teachers through the ages, he weaves life lessons through his writing which will evoke your love, make you more grateful, give you more peace, and increase your joy. This book is ultimately about you.

Rusty's book can easily be read in one sitting. It's that good. But I'll tell you how I read it. Every morning I would sit down in my favorite chair with a cup of hot tea in one hand and Rusty's book in the other, and each day I would read a new chapter in the book. It became part of my morning ritual to help me start my day more positively, gratefully, and optimistically. And it worked! Rusty's wisdom touches you like a good friend who puts his hand on your shoulder and says, "You can do it, you've got what it takes, and I love you." (I'm already encouraging Rusty to get to work on a second volume. You'll see why when you read this book.)

You are holding this book in your hands for a good reason. It's called to you. Now, embrace it, turn the page, and start reading.

I am reminded of a scene from the movie, *As Good As it Gets*, when Jack Nicholson said to Helen Hunt in a pivotal and emotional scene, "You make me want to be a better man." Rusty's book will make you want to be a better person.

I hope you enjoy reading *What We Learned From Fostering Dogs*, and I hope lots and lots of people do, too.

— David J. Pollay, Best-selling author of *The Law of the Garbage Truck* and *The 3 Promises*

Table of Contents

Preface

The Calm Before the Storm

Case of paper towels:	$36.99
Carton of bleach:	$14.59
Carton of sweeper mops:	$41.99
Two dog beds:	$34.99 each
Three-pack of dog treats:	$34.99
Thirty-two-pound bag of puppy chow:	$35.99

The girl scanning our items at the checkout in BJ's Wholesale Club didn't seem the least bit fazed by our purchase (maybe because our shopping experience wasn't all that unusual to her?). So, my wife, Elissa, decided to break the ice.

"We're going to be foster parents for two puppies. They're arriving here this weekend."

"Oh, that is so great of you guys!" the girl responded. After a brief silent pause, the young woman added, "I would love to do something like that, but I don't think I could ever let them go once I loved them. Even for a little while."

More silence followed as the last remaining items were scanned.

Elissa spoke up and said that, of course, it would be challenging, but she thought we could do it. As Elissa explained this, I took out my debit card and looked at the total on the register screen. I thought that giving them up for adoption would be easy; but shopping for them ... not so much!

We started to walk away from the register, and the girl yelled out, "God bless you!"

Wow, that was nice. Usually, I'm the one saying that phrase to others.

I'm a retired police officer. After a lengthy law enforcement career, I became an ordained minister in 2008. Elissa spent more than three decades as a high school teacher before retiring. We are both animal lovers. We live in a small South Jersey town where our pets allow us to share *their* home with them. Adding to the mix of family love are my two sons, Matt and Corey.

In the second half of my career, I worked as a school resource officer and detective. While I was assigned to the school resource unit, I was offered the opportunity to have a bomb dog. Boomer, a black Labrador retriever, and I worked together for seven years before he had to retire. He was more than a pet. He was my partner. In the fall of 2009, we had to put Boomer down because his kidneys were failing, and he had stopped eating.

Watching the euthanasia medication take effect on my canine partner of seven years would have brought me to my knees, but I was already lying on the floor with him, holding him long after his body became limp. Some call it "an act of love," but this felt anything but loving. I knew it was the right thing to do because Boomer had been suffering. That was of little comfort to me at the time, and I battled feelings of guilt, wondering if I had done the right thing.

We arrived back at the house from the veterinarian's office, and I went right to bed. Even though Boomer had stopped sleeping with us long ago, something felt empty in the house. It was as if his presence was known to me every night. I felt it in our home as we slept in bed, and he slept next to us on the floor. And now that he wasn't there, I felt his absence. I couldn't see it, but I could feel it. Perhaps you can relate.

We were now a one-dog family with Elissa's dog, Bosco, and I thought that would be enough for me. I didn't want to go through what had just happened ever again. The loss of Boomer had been too hard.

Three weeks later, we were driving home from a farm about an hour from our home with a yellow lab puppy sitting on Elissa's lap. So much for my resolve to never have to go through saying goodbye to another pet. We named this pup Bailey, and Bailey and Bosco got along great. Bailey also learned how to get along with our two cats, Bellagio and Bojangles, although this could still be considered a work in progress.

In the summer of 2012, we had to say goodbye to Bosco. Heart-wrenching doesn't come close to the feeling inside the veterinarian's office and on the way home. Watching my wife—my best friend and soul mate—grieve over losing a pet she had since before we met was hard. It was God awful, and that feeling hung in the air in our home for weeks. Hurt, no matter the source, is still pain. And this pain stung. It triggered the sting of hurt I had felt when I said goodbye to Boomer, my canine partner, a few years earlier.

Eventually, it returned to normal, and we began adjusting to the changes in the house. We were now back to just one dog, and both of us were good with that. One dog equals one food bowl, one dog leash, one load of poop (or perhaps two or three), and one dog equals only one smelly wet dog to take care of after a walk in the rain.

One dog means only one dog lying in bed with us. Of course, the upside to more than one dog is that it increases your chances of blaming one of them when you fart. But since Elissa had already professed her love to me, I wasn't worried about her leaving me because of my farts. On the other hand, Matt and Corey, my sons, I was not so sure about. However, one of the benefits of having kids is that if the dog is not around or you don't have a dog, you can always blame one of the kids for those farts!

If the word "fart" offends you, and especially the smell of them, you might want to stop reading now. Yes, I am an ordained minister, but it is best to keep things real (as Dr. Phil would say). Farts are a part of life, and if you have or will ever have a dog, you know that farts are part of that experience. Let's face it, sometimes life just stinks.

Life can get stinky at times, and your house can get stinkier as well, especially when a bunch of dogs are living in it with you. If you have a stinky home but no dogs, who could you blame it on? Seriously, if your house smells like wet dog, but has no dogs in sight, there are not a lot of options, are there?

When I was living in an apartment before Elissa and I got married, it was just Boomer and me. Besides keeping me company, he was an excellent alibi for whatever smells were in the apartment. It is unimaginable the lies I would have had to come up with if Boomer had not been there when unexpected guests stopped by and the apartment smelled.

Whether you are a dog person or not, there is no denying the fact that life gets stinky sometimes. Sometimes life gets downright crappy. But that's a topic for a later chapter. I wish I could sugarcoat it and make it sound less harsh, but that's just another facet of life you cannot avoid. Life can be harsh, and it can stink. I doubt I'm the only one who has ever believed it can get crappy at times. You don't have to look that far to see it. Just turn on the news and I bet you will not have to wait more than five minutes before a story comes on from a talking head discussing something in life that more than one of us would agree stinks.

Do you want to know what is not stinky or crappy? Love.

Unconditional love is something that we are called to share with one another. The Greek name for this kind of love is *agape*. Roughly translated into English, it means unconditional love. I cannot think of an animal, any animal, that offers that kind of love more than a dog. We, as humans, are meant to be the ones leading by example, but turn on your favorite news channel to see how we are not.

So, where do we turn if we cannot trust the evening news to share stories of unconditional love? Where do we turn to learn about this love? Where do we turn to witness this kind of love? Try Googling "quotes about the love of a dog" or "lessons learned from dogs." The first search would reveal more than 45,600,000 results; the second search would give you more than 38,500,000 results. It seems there is something special about the love of a dog, wouldn't you agree?

Would you like to find out what that kind of love looks like in people? Go to your local animal shelter and look at what the volunteers do there. Take a walk past the cages and let your heart feel what the people who routinely clean those dog runs feel in their hearts. Take a peek into the medical room and imagine what it must be like when a veterinarian takes a needle filled with a lethal dose of a barbiturate and injects it into the vein of a dog whose death sentence was set simply because he wasn't adopted.

To get a sense of what the human side of "agape love" looks like, you need to travel no further than your local animal shelter.

The word "euthanasia" comes from the Greek words that mean "good death" (a death with a minimum of suffering or distress). Some folks who have had a pet call it the last act of love, the most heart-wrenching kind of love imaginable. Have you ever been there? What if you took a moment right now and went back to that point in time in your mind's eye. Recall that day or those days if you've had more than one pet who had to be put to sleep.

Does the thought of that goodbye bring tears to your eyes? As I write this, I have a lump in my throat and tears welling up in my eyes.

Did a wound open for you that should not have been opened? If we are going to be honest about things in life, we shouldn't shy away from the bad. Sure, focusing on the good is often the best path to take, but I think we need to visit the bad times to appreciate the good times more. I think it is healthy. So, I promise you this from the bottom of my heart: As you cry, I will be crying, and as you laugh, I will be laughing. I will dig deep to reach those feelings to see what they have done to us and for us, to help you and me understand that with love comes heartache. "We ache so much because we loved so much," a wise pastor once said at a funeral service.

We would like to love and be loved without running the risk of being hurt or hurting another. I don't think we can have it that way. We want to love and feel loved, but in doing so, we have to open ourselves up to be hurt. To love something deeply (perhaps the way a person or animal deserves), we must be willing to hurt deeply. Otherwise, that love is not honest, it's holding back, and sooner or later, that kind of love becomes problematic. It does not last, does it?

We have to acknowledge that sometimes love hurts. The song *Love Hurts* made it to the Top 10 in 1975, thanks to Nazareth, taking The Everly Brothers' 1960 song and turning it into an international hit some fifteen years later. Yes, I am one of those "classic rock" people who believe the best music ever made was recorded when I was in my teenage years. I was a freshman in high school when that hit from Nazareth was played at the school dances. You do the math.

Other than going near the topic of euthanasia, have you ever done something out of love that you knew would cause pain? Discipline, maybe? How about taking a splinter out of your child's foot? You knew it had to be done, and yet you knew that you would first cause pain getting the tweezers far enough in to grab that splinter. Did you ever need stitches? Perhaps the medical folks call them sutures because stitches sound like you've gone to a seamstress instead of the emergency room.

Like the needle they inject inside the laceration to numb it, or the orange junk they pour over it and into it to disinfect it, or that scrubber that has a sponge on one side and bristles on the other; none of these is a pleasant experience.

Perhaps you had wished the doctor would just put a big, padded bandage on your boo-boo and send you on your way! That would be less painful, wouldn't it? But what would the result be? Infection is the first word that comes to my mind. To make sure you and I don't end up with something far worse than we went to the emergency room to be treated for, we had to endure some pain before things got better.

When our actions are motivated by the kind of love that is concerned for the welfare of another, sometimes we have to be the cause of pain. Other times we find ourselves being the recipients of pain. In both cases, however, the intention behind the pain is love—unconditional love. Like the folks at your local animal shelter, their rewards are intrinsic—that is, it is personal instead of something tangible, like money.

Money can be pissed away, but the feeling inside one's heart knowing they have helped someone who was in need cannot. It's not that everything previously discussed cannot put one in a pissy mood; anything that can bring feelings of delight also has the potential to piss you off. Have you ever been there? One minute you are experiencing life's bliss, and the next minute you find yourself so frustrated that you could just spit (as my mom used to say).

It's in the spirit of this myriad of feelings and emotions that this book was written. This is just the beginning, just a hint of what is waiting for you in the following pages.

Take a look at the first line of the *Prayer of Saint Francis*. I wonder how many times that first line has been prayed by people just like you and me, people who did not consider what it means to be used as an instrument of God.

Let's continue, shall we?

As we took more puppies into our home,
dinnertime became an adventure.

1

Lord make me an instrument of your peace
MOE AND LARRY

Did you ever ask for something and then later, after it arrived, thought that what you had asked for might not have been the best decision you made? Perhaps you have heard the phrase, "Be careful what you ask for." When we ask God "to be used," we have to be willing to accept all the consequences of that request. Take the first line in this oft-repeated prayer: *Prayer of Saint Francis.*

I'm the first to acknowledge that I did not know a whole lot about Saint Francis of Assisi. For a long time, the only thing I knew about him was that he was the patron saint of animals, and every year, around the first week in October, there were ceremonies blessing animals.

I don't think you need to be a Catholic in order to understand the meaning of the prayer, basically dedicated to this man from Assisi, who gave up everything he had to start preaching to ordinary people in his town of Assisi and the surrounding countryside. I don't think you even need to believe in any certain faith or religion to appreciate the words and their meaning. In fact, I don't think you need to believe in *anything* or accept any teaching to see how the idea of these words can affect change in the world.

Even if you had not previously known the prayer, I will bet there is a good chance you have heard some kind of reference to the first line: "Lord, make me an instrument of your peace." Can you see what's going on here? Imagine what it means. Giving it all up to be used by someone (even *if it is* God) is not something that comes naturally to us humans. But, oh, how lives have been changed when a few folks did submit to that kind of love. And make no mistake, this is an act of love on both ends—on the asker of this request and the giver as well.

I get that this is all about love, but why did the writer use the word *instrument?* What comes to mind when you think of the word *instrument?* If you have a word processing program on your laptop, you can find synonyms for this word, and what you get are more words like *tool, device, utensil,* and my favorite: "A thing of implementational value." Now you've got to admit, that sounds pretty important—a thing of implementational value.

What do you see in your mind when you think of any of those definitions that are synonymous with instrument? What tool comes to your mind? What kind of device are you picturing? Is the utensil one you find in the kitchen? And what about my favorite synonym? How many "things of implementational value" can you think of?

Or are you a traditional type of person, and you are sticking with the word instrument? A musical instrument? If you learned percussion in music class when you were young, like me, you are probably picturing a double bass drum set with a Slingerland snare and Zildjian cymbals (maybe one of them is a cool "sizzle cymbal"). If you were not a drummer in a garage band while you were in high school, you might be thinking of another type of musical instrument.

Getting back to this first line of the prayer, our culture and society do not take too kindly to the idea of being used. When we think of people who use others in their lives, our blood starts to boil. Okay, maybe that's just me. I just have no time for people who use others for their own gain. I don't care for people who act kind and caring when it suits them so that they can ask a favor and then drop that person (or persons) when they are done with them; once the need has been fulfilled.

It's one thing to watch it happen to someone else, especially if that person is someone we care about, like a family member, close friend, or colleague. I bet I am not alone in recalling a situation where I watched this. It's not easy to watch. But when *we're the ones* being used, well, that just makes us feel lousy. We feel foolish when we find out just how much we were used, do we not? We get mad, resentful, maybe even vengeful. And those feelings are not good for us. We know that. We know we are supposed to forgive those who hurt us. Like in *The Lord's Prayer*: "Forgive us our trespasses (or "debts," depending on your church) *as we forgive those who trespass against us* [emphasis mine]."

No one wants to look like a fool. None of us wants to be taken advantage of. So what was behind this line of the prayer? What's it trying to convey? Maybe being used in the early twentieth century (1912 is as far as the original form of this prayer can be traced) didn't have the same negative connotation that it has today? Maybe prayer was different back then?

Maybe it wasn't.

What if this is more than a prayer? What if it was suggesting putting prayer into action, putting *love* into action? St. Francis believed that nature itself was the mirror of God, and all creatures were his "brothers" and "sisters." He even preached to the birds and reportedly persuaded a wolf to stop attacking locals if he promised to feed it. Could the man who left his family's wealth (from his father's silk business) behind in order to preach the power of love have influenced a prayer that was written well after he died? Was something greater in mind other than this prayer being just a talking point for sermons?

When we think of love, we think of how it makes us feel, and how actions can turn a bad day good. But when we ask God to use us, this idea of love changes. It is not so much about how we're made to feel, but what we are doing to share our gifts. This giving of love not only changes the person receiving the love. Whatever act of love it is, it also changes the giver of love. And it can really change the giver in ways they never imagined, especially if the giver asked to be used as an instrument.

Think about it: Once used, an instrument is never the same. Whatever list of tools, devices, or utensils you came up with, picture them—each one of them—brand new. You just bought it, and it just arrived at your home. Maybe it's even still in its original packaging. Got it? Good!

Now, imagine that "thing of implementational value" just before using it. As soon as you touch it, it is forever changed. Whether from the oil on your fingers to its depreciation, once it is taken out of its wrapper, the thing you are now holding has been changed. Now go ahead and use it as it was made to be used. If it's a hammer, there are going to be nicks in it where the head came in contact with a nail; a spatula, there will be sear marks where it came in contact with the pan or the grill; a harmonica, there will be scratch marks from your teeth; if you imagined a medical instrument like a pair of forceps, they are going to need to be sterilized again. Now go ahead and think about what you first imagined and how it has been changed from the first use. No matter what I'm thinking or what you're thinking, the item(s) pictured in our heads are forever changed once they are used.

What would happen if all of the tools, devices, and utensils had a voice and said they did not want to be used? What if the hammer somehow was alive and refused to be swung? The spatula said it was not going near that hot surface? A pair of forceps got queasy at the sight of blood and did not want to go into that heart that was opened up in the operating room? What would our world look like if all the tools said they wouldn't be used? What would our world look like if all the instruments refused to be played? What would happen if every type of utensil ever invented just sat there on counters in homes, still wrapped in the plastic cocoons that kept them clean?

I can't imagine a world where all the things in it did not want to be used as they were intended. I can't imagine what my life would look like. If a hammer could talk, would it complain that it would get a splitting headache if it was used as intended (getting banged again and again into an iron nail)? If the harmonica had a voice, would it complain about someone using it so bad that it sounded horrendous? What if all the spatulas said they refused to get burned? Or the forceps, would they complain they did not want to get blood on them?

I wonder what would be more distressing: if these things were made but never used, or never made in the first place.

When we are asking to be used, as in the opening line of the *Prayer of Saint Francis*, we are asking to be transformed, being turned into something we never were before that moment in time. And once we agree, we will never be the same again. Are we ready for that? Are we ready for that kind of change *to us*?

When we agree to be used, there is a good chance it is going to cause some headaches along the way. We might get burned. Things might sound horrible. And we might get our hearts broken. Again and again. And again. But does that mean we shouldn't try? Does that mean we shouldn't take that risk? What about all these questions—and more—with a bunch of dogs thrown in the mix?

When I agreed to foster one little puppy, I was told that is all we would have in our house—just one cute puppy. I had agreed to be used, not by God, but by an organization that needed homes for dogs that would either spend their lives in a shelter or be put to sleep. This organization rescues dogs and then fosters them (in volunteers' homes) until they get adopted. The foster volunteers take care of them as if they are their own and treat them as such. If you live in a home that already has a dog (or two) in it, the fun multiplies exponentially.

When I said I agreed to be used, I probably should have said *we* agreed to be used. Elissa and I agreed to be foster parents. In essence, we agreed so that a dog might have a chance at life. Little did we know that "one little puppy" would turn into years of fostering dozens of dogs!

> *"Every boy should have two things: a dog, and a mother willing to let him have one."*
> — Jenna Schaffer

How It All Began

Elissa and I are animal lovers, and we have both been animal lovers for as long as we can remember. We grew up with pets. We even did a stint volunteering at a wildlife refuge in our town for a little while. As a teacher, my wife helped the advisor of her school's Animal Welfare Club, a club of students who find projects to help animals. One of their annual events was an adoption fair. Various animal rescues would come from all over the area to showcase their adoptable pets. It was at that event that I was invited.

My wife wanted company. I wanted to sleep in on that cold and damp October Saturday morning. So, being the man of the house, I put my foot down, demanded to be heard. And, as King of the Castle, I set the rules—just like every other husband!

After I got done telling her I was not going, I got dressed and got in the car. Well, at least I think she heard me.

The adoption fair was set up in the school's parking lot. Thank God the custodians opened the doors to the school for restroom accessibility. Once we got there, that's where I spent the first part of the morning. No, not in the bathroom, inside the school, walking around trying to stay warm. This was the same school I had graduated from and where I was now a school resource officer. I had the master key to the entire school—every door, every office, every room, even the cafeteria. We were in such a rush to get out the door that I had forgotten my keys. I was at the mercy of the custodians, who, by the way, do not get nearly enough credit for all that they do.

I was so cold I was tempted to grab a broom and work alongside one of the custodians who asked me what I was doing up so early on a Saturday morning. I explained to him that I had told my wife in no uncertain terms that I was not going to this event with her. He looked at me and, for a moment, no words were necessary; each one of us knew what the other was thinking. He just nodded at me with a sorrowful look on his face, and then he mumbled something about us all being in the same boat. As he walked out of sight, I noticed something was missing in his step: he was slower, his head hung low, the strokes of his broom were nothing like when I first saw him approaching me down the hall. I think I opened a wound that many husbands feel, and now I felt bad about it. I knew there was nothing I could do. This type of wound cannot be healed by words, it takes time. I dedicated the rest of the morning to him, a lone custodian pushing a broom down the hallway of life.

I didn't want to risk ruining anyone else's morning, so I bundled up and headed outside. As luck would have it, I arrived out there just in time to enjoy the goodies that came from Dunkin Donuts. In life, timing is everything.

After two cups of coffee (in addition to the two I had before we left the house), I headed back inside. This time it would not be to wander the halls of this sacred educational institution. I had a more pressing (and urgent) need to take care of. The bathroom was warm, warmer than the hallways. I didn't want to leave. But I had to go back outside in the cold, gray world.

As soon as I got to the table where my wife had set up, I ran into a former student. Now a young lady, she was running one of the rescues in attendance. She and Elissa were talking, and three guesses what they were talking about. Yep, my wife could not come up with *one reason* why we should not be a foster family for a rescue organization like this one. Not only did I know this young woman, but I also knew her father, a teacher. He stood next to this young lady, encouraging Elissa to go along with the scheme that was being plotted. It was almost as if the stars and planets had aligned, and fate was working against me. By the time we left the event, cell phone numbers and email addresses were already exchanged. We were told as soon as the next transport of dogs arrived, we would be the first ones called.

Less than two weeks later, my phone rang. I saw who it was. I wanted to let it go to voicemail, but my finger hit the answer button anyway. It was her, Taryn, the young lady I met when she was a high school student, the young lady whose father I knew, the young lady who had convinced my wife to get us involved in fostering a dog. There was no turning back now.

I was told to be at her house that upcoming weekend. The transport would be arriving Sunday in the late afternoon, and we would get an exact time a few hours before the dogs arrived. It was now game time. It was time to hit the stores and go shopping for what we needed—or thought we needed. So off we went to the big discount store for supplies. As we carried our purchases into the house, we looked at each other and laughed. What had we gotten ourselves into?

"We keep moving forward, opening new doors, and doing new things, because we're curious and curiosity keeps leading us down new paths."
—Walt Disney

Just before dinner that Sunday, we were officially designated as a foster family for a shelter dogs. Yes, you read that right – it's not a typo. It should have been singular, so I used the *a* to denote a singular item. However, we ended up with two puppies, so I ended the sentence with the plural form of the word, *dogs*. Technically, the entire sentence is correct because we should have been driving home with one puppy. All I did was combine what I was expecting with what actually happened. Kind of like the way you read the sentence: You were expecting it to end with proper grammar, instead you got something you weren't expecting. Now we're even.

Two new puppies in our home would be baptism by fire. They were greeted by our yellow lab, Bailey. We were not sure how she would handle the situation, but lucky for us, she saw the puppies as more of a nuisance than a new type of canine snack food with legs.

Before we left Taryn's house, we were told their names. Apparently, it's not good for foster "parents" to name the dogs they are fostering, as this leads to a situation called "foster failure." It starts with the foster family falling in love with the dog, and then instead of allowing other people to come over and see if they like the dog and want to adopt it, they end up adopting the dog themselves. When a family falls in love with the temporarily placed puppy, they often cannot bring themselves to say goodbye to the dog because they fall in love with it. So, they "fail" at "fostering," and the foster family becomes a foster failure. It all begins with the family identifying with the dog by giving it a name.

What is in a name, anyway? I guess it is part of who we are; it is who we identify ourselves as. We're given a name at birth, and then we are stuck with it. Take my name, for instance. My dad's name was Russell, his dad's name was Russell, so I was named Russell. But we all had different middle names, so at least there were no juniors, seconds, or thirds. To differentiate it from my dad's name and his dad's name, I was Rusty. Not Russ, that was my dad's name. His dad was also Russ. Such a mature-sounding name, is it not?

A name really does help give us our identity, doesn't it? Like it or not, unless we go through some legal red tape to change our names, we are stuck with the name our parents give us for eternity. In a nutshell, it is who we are. In the Christian faith, when an infant is baptized, the officiant asks the parents, "What name have you given this child?" And many ministers (including me) take that opportunity to remind everyone in attendance that the service of baptism helps serve to remind us of not who we are but *whose* we are. It is at that moment that many Christian denominations believe that the baptized are claimed as Christ's own forever. In essence, parents and sponsors of the infants are told that we change from who we are to *whose we are*.

It is at the moment that a dog gets a name that it really becomes the owner's; it belongs to the owner. It changes from just being a dog to having an identity. When we name a pet, we claim it as our own. We take on a tremendous responsibility. We assume both the risks and the rewards of being a pet owner. More often than not, we fall in love with one of God's creatures. It is very hard to let go of something you are in love with. That may be one of the reasons most rescue organizations do not want their foster families naming the animals coming into their homes.

So, we didn't get to name the two little terrier mixes that we had picked up earlier that afternoon. Their names were decided before we got there. They were two of a litter of three that came in the transport. We took two and another family—their first time at fostering as well—took the other one. We got Moe and Larry, and the other family got Curly. I guess if there were a couple more in the litter, they would have been named Shemp and Joe.

Moe and Larry were less than three months old, and they were loveable and cute. They were scared. Imagine being put in a cage, placed in a van, and driven for hours on end to a place you were not familiar with. No one told you what was going on, and you didn't know anyone when you finally got to where you were headed. You were not alone. There were dogs from other shelters in that van with you, picked up along the way to where you were now sitting. Maybe a few of us would describe that journey as exciting, but for most of us, I bet words like *scared* and *afraid* are closer to how we would be feeling.

That is just the way Moe and Larry acted when they came into our home—scared and afraid, especially when they saw a seventy-pound dog looking at them! But Bailey was great, and within a few minutes, she wanted to play with Moe and Larry out back in the yard. They ran around outside together, playing with a ball and with Bailey being chased by two little ankle-biters and the two ankle-biters being chased by Bailey. And boy, did they play! They ran around for a long while before we brought them all in for a bath.

The transport to Taryn's house was long, and being puppies, they couldn't "hold it" for the entire trip. We wiped them down as best we could at Taryn's, but they needed to be degreased. We used Dawn dishwashing detergent on them to get rid of the grime from the shelter and the urine and feces from their crates on the ride here. After a round of Dawn, we switched to puppy shampoo for that "just out of the shower, fresh scent" that any dog would long for. Bailey was shampooed first, followed by the foster puppies. Bailey, being a Labrador retriever, loves water. She is one of those dogs who loves having baths.

Imagine a wet, yellow lab running around a bathroom chasing two puppies who have never been to the second floor of a home they were now locked in. Then imagine a school teacher standing in a bathtub waiting for two puppies to be handed to her. Picture two puppies, shivering because of fear, standing in the bathtub with this teacher who is now trying to calm them down. They finally got calm enough to have lukewarm water poured over them, thereby initiating them to their first bath.

As the soap began to turn to lather, Bailey decided she wanted in on the fun. Right up and over the sidewall and into the tub, she went. Now your mind should be envisioning a woman (a cute one, if I do say so myself), two scared puppies, and a half-dry (or half-wet, depending on your point of view) yellow Labrador retriever all trying to fit in a standard size bathtub. Add some water, a little more soap thrown in for good measure, and you should have a fairly clear picture of what it looked like the first part of that first night with Moe and Larry.

"First you learn a new language, profanity; and second you learn not to discipline your dogs when you're mad, and that's most of the time when you're training dogs."
—Lou Schultz, trainer of Alaskan Huskies

But wait, there's more! As Bailey was in the middle of her second bath, she decided that it would be a good time to run out of the bathroom to get her favorite chew toy, an antler. We use deer and elk antlers for chew toys instead of rawhides because they are safer than most other chew-toy products. The only unsafe issue with this: she buries her antlers in the covers of our bed.

In an effort to keep Moe and Larry in the bathroom, I swung the door closed; it didn't latch, but at least the puppies, who were soaking wet and still covered with foamy puppy shampoo, would not escape to run through the house. After Bailey found her antler, she brought it to show to the puppies. She bounced into the bathroom, antler in mouth, as proud as anything, sitting directly in front of the tub, her tail wagging back and forth on the floor, just waiting to be acknowledged. Just as she got the attention of Moe and Larry, Bojangles, our cat, ventured into the bathroom to see what all the commotion was. Bailey nudged the door open when she came back in with her antler, and before I could reach over and pull it shut, Bojangles, sauntered in.

Take a guess at what happened next when Moe and Larry saw Bojangles? When these two soaking and soap-slathered wet puppies saw a cat for the first time in their lives, they jumped out of the tub to chase the cat with the Lab in hot pursuit. The drenched high school teacher was right on their heels.

Bojangles headed for high ground—our bed—with the three dripping canines right behind him. The puppies were not big enough to make that jump, but Bailey, on the other hand, had no problem at all. As Moe and Larry jumped up and down on their hind legs trying to get a glimpse of this creature they had never seen before, Bailey was trying to get Bojangles to play with her. On our bed. Soaking wet. Instead of playing, Bojangles leaped for Elissa's dresser along the opposite wall. Bailey was smart enough not to try it. Now two puppies were jumping up against the dresser, which Elissa inherited from her mother. Elissa, with soapy lather dripping from her chin, was now yelling at the puppies to stop scratching her mom's dresser. Bailey went back and got her antler and settled in our bed. I stood there, bent over in laughter. I would later be counseled on how I could have helped out a little more.

I figure someone had to keep a calm head about them, and I decided I was the man for that job. So I grabbed Moe and carried him back to the bathroom. Elissa got Larry and met me in there. Bailey decided to stay in bed enjoying her antler, perhaps enjoying the feel of our bedspread drying her wet fur. We decided that since she was already soaked, Elissa would jump back in the tub, and I would hand her one puppy at a time. Moe and Larry were finally rinsed and dried as best as we could with the towels that had been hanging next to the tub, towels that were now so wet they could have been wrung out. We opened the door slowly, tentatively, worrying Bojangles might still be nearby. After we saw that the coast was clear, we scooted Moe and Larry out of the bathroom, where they were met by Bailey, who jumped off the bed to join them. Elissa looked at the bathroom. I wasn't sure if they were tears of sorrow or tears of joy. The walls were soaked, the floor was soaked, wet dog hair clung to every surface, and clumps of it were scattered along the bottom of the tub. Herding squirrels would have been easier.

Next up, dinner (this time for three dogs, not just one). How would Bailey handle this? My former partner, Boomer, was food aggressive and had to be fed separately from Bosco. Moe and Larry combined did not weigh as much as Bosco. If Bailey wanted to, she could make our two foster dogs a tasty Scooby Snack. Now, for the first time since they came into our house, I was nervous.

Bailey assumed her normal position in the kitchen as Elissa prepared dinner for the dogs. No dinners were being prepared for the humans in the house. You see, Elissa believes in spoiling a pet, and if that means making them dinner to go along with their pet food, so be it. Ever since we got married, I witnessed the ritual of Elissa cooking chicken for the dogs. The baked chicken (most of the time rotisserie-cooked) was added to and mixed in with the dog food. It was only after that blending of various foods came together that the bowl was ready to be placed on the floor.

It turned out Bailey didn't care if two puppies were eating near her or next to her; she didn't bother with their bowls of food. However, the same could not be said about Larry and Moe. They scarfed down their food like it was their last meal and then went straight to Bailey's bowl. Bailey didn't show her teeth or growl. She just backed away and let them finish what she left. She looked up at us as if to say, "Are you serious?"

Elissa snuck Bailey a few pieces of chicken before she put it back in the fridge to make things even. This was when I saw my extensive dog experience as a benefit to the family. I knew that after you got done feeding puppies, there was only one thing to do: Put them outside! So back outside the three of them went, and back to the playing and chasing each other in the yard. I stood out there with them while Elissa cleaned up their bowls and started preparing our meal. I was hoping Bailey would lead by example—that is, she would show them what they were supposed to do after dinner. I lost sight of them quite a few times and assumed that the outdoor time was being used well. I assumed they wanted some privacy to "do their business" and called them up on the deck after about fifteen minutes. They had their fall coats on, and I was dressed in a t-shirt. No one ever said the desire to get warm is not a good motivator.

"My husband and I are either going to buy a dog or have a child.
We can't decide whether to ruin the carpets or ruin our lives."
—Rita Rudner

Once inside the back door, Moe went over to Elissa, seemingly hoping for another bite of chicken. When she didn't give it to him, he squatted down and peed at her feet as she was cutting garlic. Larry, not to be outdone, went into the family room and took a dump. Bailey looked at both of them, then at us, and walked away into the living room. I guess she was disgusted with everything that had just gone down. We didn't have time to play *rock, paper, scissors* to decide who would clean up what. We simply went by who was closest to whatever mess. I was closest to Larry; Elissa was almost standing in Moe's urine. Instead of paper towels that wouldn't flush down the toilet, I ran into the bathroom and grabbed a handful of toilet paper. Elissa was busy with the roll of paper towels taking care of the kitchen spill. I headed for the family room, game plan in hand.

Did you ever think you had enough of something only to find out you actually didn't? In trying to continue to stay environmentally friendly, I took what I thought would be just enough toilet paper from the roll hanging on the wall next to the toilet. It turns out I was wrong. My estimates put it wrong by a good ten to twelve sheets. This was a two-ply roll.

Either I did not grab enough toilet paper, or the load of crap was bigger than I thought. Now looking back at it, I cannot believe something that big came out of a dog that small. Either way, by the time I realized that I had miscalculated the whole thing, it was too late. I reached down with the layers of toilet paper in my hand, determined to grab the entire pile in one squeeze of my hand. Again, it turned out I was wrong. Instead of grabbing the entire pile, I got maybe three-quarters of it in my hand. There was one more thing I miscalculated: its moisture content.

Now I was standing, my right arm outstretched, the palm of my right hand facing up. In that hand held the key to this entire operation. If I made it to the bathroom, I would be a hero (at least in my mind), and if I didn't make it to that most sacred of all rooms in any man's domicile, I would be a complete failure. I didn't even make it halfway down the hallway before I started losing it. And I do mean, losing it! Not only did I lose some of the material that was in my hand, but I was also losing my stomach right along with it. This mistake that I was set on cleaning up was wetter than I thought. If you know anything about toilet paper, even the good stuff is no match for moisture. As globs of Larry's fecal waste were falling along either side of my wrist, I could feel the gooiness of it seeping into the palm of my hand. So yeah, I was literally losing it.

Let's see, did I miss anything so far? Yes. The smell of it. I don't know why I thought running down the hall would be better than walking, but it seemed like the right thing to do at the time. Just like the position I held my hand, it was up around chest level, right out in front of me. That means that the odor wafted gently past my nose because it was at almost the same height. So the faster I ran, the faster it sped into my nostrils. Dry heaves for everyone!

I do apologize for this part, these last couple of descriptive paragraphs. Perhaps it should have come with a disclaimer of a sort: Warning, do not try this at home. However, may I offer one tip that has not been touched upon yet? Open the lid to the toilet before you begin. That should be the first step.

What had been anticipated as a genius solution on my part to a particularly messy problem turned into a messier problem for Elissa to contend with. I was heaving so hard by this point that she felt terrible for me and cleaned up the family room on her own. And the hallway. And the toilet lid, toilet bowl, and top of the tank. And the walls.

We had not been home more than three hours, and already the house was a disaster. But that's okay. It's the sacrifices we make for those who are in need. It's the pain we endure without complaining. It's the price of doing business when that business involves being used as an instrument.

No one has asked what Moe and Larry were doing while all the aforementioned fun was going on. They were in the living room with Bailey, chewing on the leg of the sofa.

Yes, there is a price, isn't there?

But there is Good News. We are given the chance again and again and again to change and to be changed. The offer is there for us to be used—not for our own good or purpose, but for a greater good and a higher purpose. We can be part of something bigger than ourselves. But it has to start somewhere, and it has to start sometime. Is not today as good a day as any?

Larry on the left and Moe on the right.

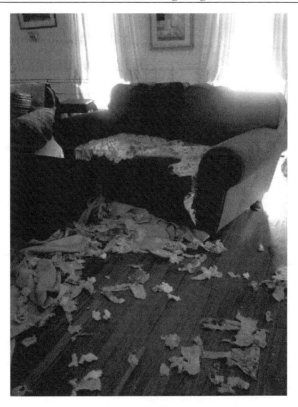

It's amazing what two puppies can accomplish in a
relatively short period of time.

2

Where there is hatred, let me sow love
ROCKY AND EIKO

B uddha is quoted as saying, "Hatred does not cease by hatred, but only by love; this is the eternal rule." A senior pastor once asked his congregation, "What does love look like?" In 1984, Tina Turner recorded the hit song, "What's Love Got to Do with It?" and seventeen years before that, the Beatles recorded "All You Need is Love."

It is easy to find quotes, songs, and themes about love. Try doing the same for hatred. I will save you time because you will not have much luck. Sure there are a few quotes with the word in it, more songs with hate in a lyric or two, but you will not find many positive themes in your search if you are looking for stuff on hate. Rightly so, because there is a real negative connotation with that word. It evokes strong feelings.

Depending on what version of the Bible you are reading, the word *love* is used more than two hundred times in the New Testament. Buddha was believed to have lived sometime between the fourth and sixth centuries BCE. That means the idea that love is greater than hate goes back hundreds of years before Jesus walked on this earth. Millions of copies of the Prayer of St.

Francis were distributed both during and immediately after World War II by a Catholic cardinal from New York and a US senator from New Jersey. The sixties were filled with songs about love (and love itself), and Ms. Turner was one of many singers to bring that theme into the later parts of the twentieth century. Now, two decades into the twenty-first century, we're still surrounded by the very idea of love (and equality).

It would seem love really does cover a multitude of sins (paraphrasing 1 Peter 4:8). One of my sins is not eating vegetables. I'm not sure I will ever get to *love* them. In fact, I doubt I will even get to *like* them. But Elissa never got the memo on this; she insists on putting those green things in front of me at dinnertime. She is so persistent that she has even found ways to try to slip them into some of my favorite meals—her pasta dishes.

> *"My dog is half pit bull and half poodle. Not much*
> *of a watchdog, but a vicious gossip!"*
> —Craig Shoemaker

Some folks just do not have a taste for certain things, do they? And when it comes to dogs, nothing seems to polarize people like "dangerous breeds." The mention of certain breeds can cause havoc in an otherwise civil conversation. First up: the pit bull. Add a famous football player who played the quarterback position, and watch out! Talk about hatred. You either get hatred for the man or hatred of the haters who hate the man who did a stint in a correctional facility for his role in a dogfighting ring.

Before we go any further, I want to make one thing clear: this is not about judging someone. There are plenty of articles written and blogs filled with comments and opinions about that particular incident and person. For the record, I believe in forgiveness. Forgiveness does not mean you condone an act. It has nothing to do with the person being forgiven—it has everything to do with the person doing the forgiving.

Forgiveness simply means you no longer hold the person responsible for the debt *to you*. You stop looking for revenge or a payback of sorts. It is *not* condoning the act, and it is *not* sympathizing with the person. It is simply *moving on for your own good*. But we will save a deep dive into this topic for the next chapter.

If nothing else, the incident brought about conversations on the breed. The pit bull became synonymous with viciousness. People hated the dog simply because of what it was. It didn't matter where it came from, what kind of training it had, or even its temperament. All that mattered was the breed: pit bull. People who owned them tried to call them something else, pet owners who adopted them from shelters were forced to lie to their insurance companies or apartment complex managers, and newscasters and talking heads made the breed itself the story.

Many people who saw a pitbull being walked would turn and go the other way. Dog parks posted signs prohibiting them, homeowner associations banned them, and judges sentenced them to death. If all the things just mentioned are not signs of hatred, I don't know what they are. But are they signs or symptoms of hatred? As paramedics, we learned the difference between signs and symptoms of a disease or illness. Signs are physical manifestations of disease; they can be measured, like vital signs (pulse, blood pressure, rate of breathing, temperature). Symptoms are more subjective; they are what the patient experiences and have to be described (pain, nausea, itching, dizziness). Signs are definitive indications of a disease, and symptoms are characteristics of a disease or illness. Put another way, signs are observations from an objective observer, and symptoms are subjective descriptions from the point of view of the person experiencing them.

So, what about the pit bull? Think about the signs of hatred for this dog. What are the physical, tangible observations you can make? Keep them objective; what have you seen?

Now consider what symptoms of this hatred might look like. What are some of the descriptions that come to mind when thinking about it from the point of view of the hated? What would they say if they had a voice? What would they share with us? How would they feel?

Ask anyone involved with a pit bull rescue, and you will hear stories of heartache, ignorance, and finally, when the dog gets adopted, love. For those of you who have taken a chance and thrown caution to the wind with your homeowner's insurance, you know how much love this dog can give. Sure, you know how strong they are, but you also know how loveable they are.

You have to wonder what breed of dog will be demonized next by the media, and eventually society. Today it's the pit bull; before the pit bull, it was the Rottweiler; before the Rottweiler, it was the Doberman, before that it was the German shepherd. It seems our society is always looking for a scapegoat, something (or someone) to hate. Next time you are in line at the grocery checkout, glance at the headlines in the tabloids. How many of them incite some kind of hatred?

Who knew that the pit bull was once called the "nanny dog" because it was so good with children and people trusted them? Perhaps the most famous pit bull comes to us from a television show from the 1930s, *The Little Rascals* ("Our Gang Comedy"). Although he didn't have a talking part, he was a beloved character in the shows that aired once a week before the advent of color television. His name was Petey, and he was an American pit bull terrier. He didn't look so scary, did he?

In a 2010 Daily Beast website post, an article titled "The World's Most Dangerous Dogs" listed the top nineteen most vicious.

That article listed the Akita as the fourth most dangerous dog and the Belgian Malinois as the fourteenth most dangerous dog. In November of 2012, a mixed breed Akita/Belgian Malinois arrived at our house.

"He is your friend, your partner, your defender, your dog.
You are his life, his love, his leader. He will be yours,
faithful and true, to the last beat of his heart.
You owe it to him to be worthy of such devotion."
—Unknown

Being a retired bomb dog handler meant I had experience with larger breeds. In canine school, when we were not training the dogs for scent work, some of the guys who had patrol dogs wanted to spend the time in a useful way. In police work, it's called "taking hits," and it means you wrap your arm in a piece of leather or burlap and *take a hit* from a patrol dog. Roughly translated, you get all bitten up. If you are lucky, you get to wear a long, padded sleeve on your arm. You still feel the pressure of the bite, but not the intense pain from the teeth. Sometimes you stand there waiting for the patrol dog to take a running leap at you. Sometimes you are resisting arrest from the canine officer, and without having to be commanded, the dog leaps at you and holds on until you stop resisting. Other times, you get a running start, just for the fun of it, and you learn just how fast a trained police dog is. It doesn't matter what scenario you are practicing; you end up on the ground more often than not. They are that strong, fast, and tenacious.

I had been doing this fun part of canine training since before I joined the police department. When I was volunteering with the local emergency squad as an EMT, I was asked by the canine officers if I wanted to "help" them do some training. When you are a senior in high school and a couple of cops ask you to do something, you say yes without thinking about it. Thirty years of taking hits come with its share of stories. I promised not to mention a lot of them because the scars on my body were never reported to reduce paperwork. A cop is always looking for ways to get out of taking a report, even if that means buying another cop a case of beer as a way of saying, "I'm sorry for my dog chewing you up." You accept the offer.

In the short time we had been fostering (five dogs by this time), Taryn, the organization's executive director, and I shared a lot of our backgrounds. She knew my experience not only working a police dog but working with trainers (police and civilian) and judging police canine competitions. Her phone call to me was not that surprising. A dog was in a shelter in a southern state and was on their euthanasia list. He was going to be put down the next day if he wasn't pulled from the shelter immediately. Because of my background, I would be the only one asked. I asked, "Why?"

The dog in question was a ten-month-old Belgian Malinois/Akita mix and was an owner surrender. That meant his original owner did not want him anymore, so he was dropped off (surrendered) at the shelter. Because of his breed, he immediately went on the shelter's euthanasia list. Larger dogs in that part of the country do not get adopted easily, and since police departments use Belgian Malinois for canine patrol, people in that community don't like them. His chances of being adopted were slimmer than slim, and to make room for other, more adoptable dogs, he would be put to sleep as soon as the mandatory three-day wait expired. We were already at day two.

What was I supposed to say? The shelter had no information on him, no idea if he had a history of human aggression, dog aggression, or any other behavior that might make him a difficult placement. When you are told a dog will die tomorrow if you do not take him today, it's almost impossible to say no. At least for us. We figured we would deal with whatever issues he had when he got to our home. I said we would take him.

Great, he was arriving the next day. There was not much time to get ready. Up until that point, we had fostered puppies and a medium-sized dog who was docile and easygoing. They were all adopted fairly quickly. Since we had no fosters living with us, when I said yes, Taryn took that opportunity to ask one more question: Would we take one more dog from that same shelter? A hound mix had been there since he was a puppy; although not born there, he was dropped off there shortly after he was born. The icing on the cake was a picture she texted me while we were talking. It was a picture of him at the shelter. I asked Taryn if this girl was good or what.

Sure, what's one more dog? Time to get into combat mode. Who in our rescue had a large crate? Did we have any large bowls in the house? How about a large dog bed? And what about food? A seventy-five-pound Malinois/Akita mix can eat! Time to head out and do some shopping.

To be fair to Elissa, she never had a large dog; all her dogs were dogs you could carry around if you had to (or wanted to). When I came into her life with Boomer, she had already seen him working at the school where she taught. A high school bomb threat means sweeps of the school with bomb dogs. Boomer was in the school even when he wasn't working, and he got to know all the staff and students. Because I was assigned at that high school, and he was my partner, the students and teachers got to see him every day. Boomer, although big, was not intimidating to Elissa. He had endeared himself to her the first summer we were together. Elissa had decided that the hottest day of the year was the best day to weed the gardens in the front yard. Boomer went out with her and took to a shady spot on the porch. I figured if the air temperature and humidity were both in the mid-nineties, it was best to stay inside and soak up the coolness of the air-conditioning. About twenty minutes after they ventured outside, I heard Boomer barking like crazy. I got up to see what was going on and found Elissa lying on the steps, almost unconscious. Boomer was standing over her, barking to get my attention. Once inside and cooled down, I noticed that Boomer would not leave her side. He didn't leave her side from that day on. From that day on, he could do no wrong in Elissa's eyes.

But this time, things would be different. Neither one of us knew what we were getting. Elissa was concerned. She was more than concerned. She was worried. What would this dog be like? What if he and Bailey didn't get along? As big as he was—

considering his breed—she worried what he could do to Bailey if he wanted to. What if we got stuck with him because no one wanted to adopt him (again, because of his breed and appearance)? What about the other dog we were getting with him, the hound mix? What if he went after him? We had so many questions that we didn't have any answers to. I have to admit, I had some apprehension, myself. Yep, this retired cop, a former bomb dog handler who had taken hits from police canines for decades, was a wee bit nervous.

"J'embrasse mon chien sur la bouche!"
(I kiss my dog on the mouth)—Unknown author

We waited for what seemed like hours for them to arrive. A caravan of vans and SUVs were bringing in dogs from along the I-95 corridor to a family home in the Pine Barrens of southern New Jersey. Finally, they pulled up to the house, and I saw that Taryn's father, Jay, had the two we were taking home. He eased his way out of the driver's door of his pickup truck and looked at me with a sinister smile as he wiped the side of his face. Uh, oh. What had we gotten ourselves into?

Jay made his way over to the rear passenger side and looked back over his shoulder at me again. There were probably a dozen or so foster families waiting in addition to us, all of them excited about meeting their newest foster dogs. A few of them were first-timers, just like we had been a few months earlier. But it seemed like all eyes were on me. What did everyone know that I didn't know? Or were they just curious to see what this dog we were getting was all about? Maybe they had a running bet, a pool going on between just them to see how long it would be before this dog tried to eat me? Whatever was going on, it did not help alleviate any anxiety I was feeling.

As Jay opened the door, I could see a head peer out. A big head. A head bigger than any other dog head that ever arrived at that particular house since the rescue was in business. The door opened a little further, just enough for Jay to reach in and grab the leash attached to this animal's neck. One more glance in my direction, and then he opened the door all the way. Before he was even invited to come out, the Belgian Malinois/Akita mix launched himself out of the truck and almost pulled Jay over when he ran out of leash. Jay calmed him down and let him empty on a nearby bush. They began walking toward us, and then Jay stopped and told us to "Watch this." He then got down on one knee in front of this newest rescue, and we saw something amazing. All this dog wanted to do was give Jay kisses. I mean wet, sloppy kisses. This feared man-eater got on his hind legs and placed his front paws on Jay's shoulders. He then began licking his face like crazy. It was all Jay could do to get him to stop.

When the love-fest was over, it was our turn. We were told his name was Eiko, and all he wanted to do the entire trip up to New Jersey was lick Jay's face. There wasn't a crate for him, so Eiko sat in the back seat—at first. That did not last long, and Eiko enjoyed the front seat for most of the ride. Being in the front seat, he had access to the right side of Jay's face. When it was our turn to meet him, I was given the end of the leash and told, "Good luck!"

No sooner did I have the leash in my hand than Eiko jumped on my shoulders and began licking me like crazy. The more I told him to stop, the harder he licked. I started laughing, and before I knew it, I was making out with a Belgian Malinois/Akita mix. My mouth was open as I was laughing, and Eiko took that opportunity to insert his tongue down my throat. Sure, I had been accused of making out with a few "dogs" in my early days, but this was the first time it was witnessed by so many innocent people. French kissing a Belgian dog who had part of his heritage in Japan, I guess you could say I became a sort of world traveler on that afternoon.

"The dog is the most faithful of animals and would be much esteemed were it not so common. Our Lord God has made His greatest gifts the commonest."
—Martin Luther

As I was dealing with Eiko, Elissa helped unload the rest of the dogs, all of them in crates of various sizes. One of the smaller crates had a scared but friendly brindle-colored dog named Nathan. There was a brief meeting of the minds, and because he had never been out of a shelter and just needed to be given a chance, we renamed him, Rocky.

If you remember the movies by the same name, there were a few lines that involved being given a chance. In *Rocky I*, Adrian has this conversation with Paulie:

Adrian: "Einstein flunked out of school twice."
Paulie: "Is that so?"
Adrian: "Yeah. Beethoven was deaf. Helen Keller was blind. I think Rocky's got a good chance."

And in *Rocky II*, Rocky tells Adrian, "I'll drive you crazy if you give me a chance."

We decided that Nathan just needed a chance; if given the opportunity to flourish in a home instead of a shelter, he would turn out to be a good dog. In honor of the biggest underdog in American films, Nathan became Rocky on that night.

And just like that, our fears, worries, concerns, and anxieties vanished. Eiko didn't want to eat anyone. He was more concerned with licking. Rocky was a friendly dog who ran around with Eiko before jumping in our car behind him for the ride home. Just like on the ride up to New Jersey, Eiko made sure the side of our faces were slopping wet by the time we got home. It was all we could do to keep him out of our laps during that ride; he insisted on trying to convince us he was a small lap dog who deserved to be riding up front. Rocky seemed to be enjoying both his new name and the back seat, where he was chilling out while Eiko made the ride interesting.

Once home, we made sure to introduce Eiko and Rocky to Bailey slowly by way of a walk. I got out of the car first, and Elissa handed me our newest foster dogs. Rocky was unsure of himself, and he didn't seem to care much for the leash. On the other hand (literally), Eiko was full of energy and curiosity. He got up on his hind legs. Then he placed his front paws on my shoulders and looked me square in the eyes. I could not believe we were the same height.

Right there in the driveway, he started making out with me again. I wasn't sure if he was happy to be out of the shelter or this was just his nature. But the term "over-affectionate" barely scratches the surface when describing his behavior that day.

The plan was for me to take Eiko and Rocky a few doors down the street, and Elissa would go inside, hook Bailey up to her leash, and then she would meet us away from the house, in neutral territory. I guess Elissa figured I would have had plenty of time to walk to the next house before she came out the front door with Bailey. Unfortunately, Eiko had other ideas. He seemed happy to continue kissing me instead of heading down the street to christen some bushes in the neighborhood. So when Elissa came outside with Bailey, instead of being in the middle of the street, away from her line of vision, we were just a few feet from her. Things do not always go as planned.

It turned out our concern for Bailey getting territorial with a larger dog on her property was for naught. She saw Eiko as a companion. Finally having a playmate her size, she didn't have to concern herself (or us) with playing too rough or pouncing too hard. This first meeting went great for all three of them. Rocky warmed up to Bailey, who was more interested in Eiko's playfulness than his laidback personality. The walk was more like three kids trying to get to know one another on a playground. Only this time, they were hooked up to leashes.

After a walk that finally did include Eiko peeing on what seemed like every tree, bush, and shrub on the street, we headed back to the house. Once inside and off leashes, the three started running laps through the first floor: kitchen, into the dining room, through the living room, past the front door, down the hallway, and then back into the kitchen. That constituted one lap. There would be many more laps completed that evening. But we thought that a combined weight of close to two hundred pounds of canine would be better served in the backyard, so out the door they went.

This gave us time to get bowls of water down and some treats ready for when they came back in from their playtime. I am guessing about twenty minutes went by before we heard them on the deck by the back door. It had rained earlier in the day; in fact, it had been raining steadily since the night before. We tried wiping them down with towels. One at a time, they were invited inside, Rocky first. He was easy; he stood there nice and calm and let us wipe him down. It wasn't great, but at least mud wouldn't be tracked throughout the house if the laps started up again. Don't forget the furniture! Mud does not come out of sofas and chairs as easily as you might think. We had become somewhat of foster experts by this time, and we made the necessary decision to sacrifice the older furniture in the family room for the sake of saving the good furniture in the living room. We felt bad about it, but sometimes in life, you have to make decisions that involve sacrifices for the better good.

> *"Being there for a friend is one of the greatest gifts you can give. Another is allowing them to be there for you."*
> —Unknown

Eiko was next in the door. He wasn't let in like Rocky was. The door was not opened by a human to allow him to walk in. Nope, Eiko demonstrated his first act of intelligence by opening the back door himself. I guess he would decide when he was coming in, not us. He stood on his hind legs and pawed at the doorknob until it opened. We have those lever-type doorknobs throughout the house, including the exterior doors. Eiko simply pushed down on it, and the door popped open. And in he ran. He was feeling amorous to us once again. But this time, he cast his eyes toward Elissa, standing there with a wet, muddy bath towel in her hand. I think that made her look more desirable in his eyes. By the time his muddy paws landed on her shoulders, his tongue was already going to town on her face. She tried to duck, tucking her chin to her chest. This only got her scalp soaked with dog slobber as he stroked her hair with his tongue. Eiko's back paws left a path of dance steps on the kitchen floor, leaving a trail of evidence where he pushed her around the floor. It was obvious he was leading. She was screaming.

Since the back door was open, nothing was stopping Bailey from coming into the house. She created the distraction that Elissa needed to escape the love that Eiko was covering her with. When Eiko saw Bailey, he immediately let go of Elissa and ran over to her. They started playing right there in the kitchen, both still wet and both still with muddy paws, although Eiko's front paws were not as muddy as they were before he rested them on Elissa's shoulders. After shutting the door, I grabbed Eiko and Elissa took Bailey. We did our best to get the worst of the mud off them, but after taking a step back and surveying the damage, we saw that they all needed a bath.

If you remember our first bath experience with foster dogs, know that we had learned from that first disaster. We were now hardened veterans at this. We didn't go upstairs for baths anymore. We now used the first-floor shower—a walk-in shower with a shower door that closes.

The system we put in place went like this: Each dog, one at a time, would be led into the bathroom, the door immediately closed behind them. Towels would already be stacked on the toilet lid, and at least two large bath towels already spread out on the floor. Elissa would change into old clothes before the start of this. Elissa would stand at the ready in the shower (equipped with one of those hand-held shower heads with a hose that allows you to spray anywhere you want), and I would escort the dog into the stall with her. Quickly, I would close the door behind the dog and then lean against it so it couldn't be opened from the inside, preventing an unwanted escape. Elissa was charged with the task of cleaning and rinsing, and my task was to throw dry towels over the glass wall so she could dry the dog while still surrounded by shower glass. Only after said dog had been dried off would the door be opened. After finishing the job, I would grab another clean towel before opening the bathroom door to release one clean dog.

This process would be repeated until every dog was bathed. Streamlined and efficient, that's the way we did things around what had now affectionately been called the Williams' Canine Hotel. And speaking of streamlined and efficient, Bojangles and Bellagio learned a few tricks of their own since Moe and Larry had been adopted. For example, they had become experts in judging the distance needed to outrun any new foster that arrived. They developed this keen sense of awareness of exactly how far they needed to be from any given dog in the house, and that distance varied with each dog. They knew every dog was unique and quickly adopted strategies to deal with each temperament and, in particular, the speed of each foster. That continued with Eiko and Rocky.

Rocky, being the laidback dude that he was, allowed the cats to be as curious of him as he was of them. It's safe to say that they were more interested in him than he was in them. On the other hand, Eiko was *definitely* interested in what they were all about! All it took was a couple of whacks from the paws of Bojangles to his face, and Eiko decided it was safer to stick with dogs than cats.

Hey, remember when I added up the total weight of the three dogs as they were running around the house? Great, now take that and divide it evenly by the area of a queen-size bed. Add in two humans to get a mental picture of that first night with Rocky and Eiko. Just make sure you leave room for two cats who jumped onto the bed in the middle of the night. Actually, make that jumped *into* the bed in the middle of the night. Elissa awoke to find Bellagio under the covers, curled up against her legs; Bojangles took a special liking to my pillow.

There we were, one big happy family: two cats, three dogs, and two humans who had no idea how it all came to this. At least I did not have to go to work the next morning. Elissa's alarm went off as it does every morning (and has for the past thirty-five years) at 4:50 a.m. She got up, and I stayed in bed.

"As soon as you concern yourself with the 'good' and 'bad' of your fellows, you create an opening in your heart for maliciousness to enter. Testing, competing with, and criticizing others weaken and defeat you."
— Morihei Ueshiba (Founder of Aikido), *The Art of Peace*

Martin Luther King, Jr. once said, "In the end, we will remember not the words of our enemies, but the silence of our friends." I have to wonder how many of us stay silent when we should be speaking up. What holds us back from doing the right thing? Why do so many people stay silent when they witness acts of bullying?

Of all the terms that evoked feelings of fear and intimidation in the dog world, the branding "bully breed" has to be up there at the top. It was not always that way; in fact, before the 1980s, that term for dogs couldn't be found. Our society will stand by and watch the bullying of people, but just the mention of a bully breed dog, and you get folks coming out of the woodwork to speak their minds. If it is a dog that sounds scary, we want nothing of it in our community. What would our world look like if we sowed love where we saw bullying? Bullying in our schools and playgrounds as well as dogs classified as bully breeds?

Can we sow love where there is hate? Can we plant seeds of love where we see disgust? Can we put our fears aside to show love to someone (or something) who has been labeled as bad or dangerous?

It is not easy; it will not be easy. You finally take that risk, and before you know it, you are making out with a seventy-five-pound dog!

Hatred does not always have to be an overt act or statement. It can be hatred by omission. Ignorance, apathy, laziness, or even boredom are some of the ways we deal with things we're not comfortable with. When we do not understand something, we have two choices: Learn more about it, or dismiss it. One takes work, and the other involves doing nothing.

What happens when we take time to learn more about something that we don't understand? When we put our preconceived ideas aside and take it at face value? When do we not formulate an opinion until we have all the facts? What *would* (future tense) happen if we took the time?

I doubt I'm alone in searching for facts to support my opinion. Sometimes my opinion is strong, and I need as many facts as possible to engage anyone who might disagree with all the knowledge on the subject that is stored in my powerful—and all-knowing—brain. It really is easy to get caught up in ourselves, isn't it? Can you imagine what our lives would look like if we gathered all the facts *first* and then came up with our opinions? Instead of searching for only the facts that support our way of seeing something, what if we searched through *all* the available facts and then decided?

History is riddled with hatred, persecution, and oppression of people because of the way they look. Rumors (unsubstantiated) have directed actions against groups of individuals guilty of nothing other than what was told about them. Fear has driven us to wars with people from other countries who were killed because of their beliefs. Misunderstanding before knowing all the facts (a definition of prejudice) has caused more harm than could be written in all the books in all the libraries in the world. Yet it continues.

You have to wonder what dogs would say (assuming they had a voice) about us; how would they treat us if they acted on everything they heard about us? What would they say to each other about us humans if they heard all we want to do is harm them or use them for our benefit? How lucky are you and I that all a dog sees is love?

How lucky are we that we get to feel something that we never dreamed of happening? We can feel the love of one of God's creatures that just needed a chance, or the paws of a gentle giant on our shoulders. Just remember to keep your mouth closed when the love fest begins.

There is Good News for all of us, good news in the form of understanding—understanding that we do not have to look the other way, we do not have to feel compelled to go with the crowd because of fear or ignorance. You and I, we have a chance to take hatred and turn it into something special. We can turn hate into love. In doing so, we have an opportunity to demonstrate to God and our neighbors that love is more than a feeling. Love is an action.

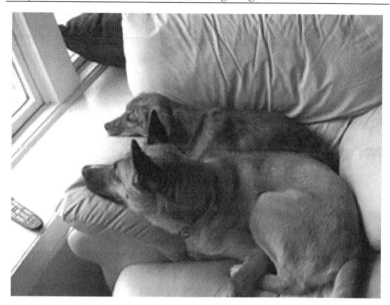

Eiko (in the foreground) and Rocky stare out the window
as they ponder life in their new home.

Eiko, the resourceful one, uses Rocky as a pillow.

3

Where there is injury, pardon

REPTAR

ver been hurt? Ever been the instigator of hurt? If you can read this, that means you are probably older than a fifth-grader. That means you've lived a life filled with joy and sorrow, sickness and health, pleasure and pain. Pleasure and pain can be the hardest, can't they? It seems like we are continually trying to find ways of grabbing one and avoiding the other. We can be the receiver of pleasure or pain, or we can be the giver.

None of us have gotten this far in life without being hurt. None of us has gotten this far in life without hurting someone. It's just the way it is. It might not be fair, but who said life is fair? Who was it that said, "Life is not the way it's supposed to be, it's the way it is"?

If you've been hurt, you may want some kind of retribution. If I've been hurt, I know I look for a day of reckoning for whoever caused the pain. Yeah, I know, as a religious man I should not be looking for revenge. I might have been ordained into the Christian ministry, but that doesn't mean I stopped being a human. I, too, am still working on things. I have a lot of baggage and have lived a lot before the whole "calling" thing happened. And I will share with you that I tried to avoid it; I looked the other way. In my first book, *Can I Get There From Here?*, I write about my experience saying "No," but God was not taking "no" for an answer. I kept insisting to God that I was the wrong guy. Eventually, I caved and took God up on the idea. At the time, I wasn't sure if God was rethinking this idea about me or not. I know I'm not, but I guess you could say I am still a work in progress

How about you? Are you still working on things in your life that would make it better? Working on things that would make you a better person? Me too! And one of them is not looking for paybacks every time I've been hurt. I'm not seeking revenge or making sure justice is served each and every time. What about you?

"To err is human; to forgive, canine."
—Unknown

Why is forgiveness so hard? We all want to be forgiven when we screw up. We all look for compassion and understanding from the one who has been hurt. Forgiveness is a theme in every major religion; it's important for society in general. Some might say it is needed for society to function at all. If we all want forgiveness, if we all feel we deserve it at some time or another, and if we all want to be the ones being forgiven, who will be the ones doing the forgiving? Imagine a world where everyone is forgiven, but no one does the forgiving.

Strange, isn't it? When I meet with couples before they get married, I ask them what would happen if someone made their future spouse look like a loser. I probe deeper and ask them how they would react if someone made their future spouse *feel* like a loser. You probably wouldn't be surprised at the answers. No one wants their loved one to look like a loser, and no one wants their partner to feel like a loser. Not one of us would stand by and allow it to happen.

After agreeing that neither person would allow that to happen, I ask them how they settle arguments. How do they get their way? I then ask them, "If you go out of your way to win every argument, what are you automatically making your partner?" After a brief pause, in that moment when they understand, I explain the futility of winning every argument. Because, in a relationship, if we are good at finding ways of winning, the opposite is also true: we are good at making the other person a loser. And we do become good at it. But if we wouldn't stand by and allow someone else to do it, why do we do it? Why do we feel we have a license to hurt the very person we are about to marry? It doesn't matter if you are in a relationship or not. You can relate this concept to those in your life that you care about. We all can. It doesn't matter if we're getting married or not. The idea of making someone we care about a loser does not sit well for most decent people.

That sums up my marital advice to couples. The rest of the time, we talk about their lives, dreams, expectations, and worries. At the end of the meeting, I give the couple a calculator, a cheap one I usually pick up on the way to the meeting (hey, I'm retired, and it's not like I have a ton of money sitting around for a nice wedding gift). Before I surrender this precious token of my hopes for them, I remove the battery from it. I suggest that they keep this calculator handy, maybe leave it in a conspicuous place in their home. And I tell them to never put a battery in it, never even think about turning it on. Because, I explain, if each one tries to calculate how much they are giving or how much the other owes in the relationship, it will never work. In short, don't keep score.

"Never let the odds keep you from pursuing what you know in your heart you were meant to do."
—Satchel Paige

If October mornings in New Jersey can be cold, damp, and nasty, imagine a rainy night in December. Around ten o'clock, I received a call from Taryn explaining a peculiar situation that she only trusted me with. Another dog she knew little about, one that was abandoned in a home a few towns away from ours. Once again, my background in handling large dogs and dogs with aggression issues made me the perfect foster to place this animal with. It's hard to say "No" when you hear a family has packed up and moved and left their dog tied to a tree in the backyard.

The deal Elissa and I had by this time was that neither would agree to accept a dog into our home without first checking with the other and discussing it. But the tone of Taryn's voice told me this was, quite literally, a "do-or-die" situation, and before I could say, "Let me check with Elissa," I heard the following words come out of my mouth: "I'll meet you there in thirty minutes."

> Elissa: "Who was that?"
> Me: "Oh, it was Taryn."
>
> Elissa: "What did she want?"
> Me: "Huh, what?"
>
> Elissa: "What did Taryn want to discuss at this time of night?"
> Me: "Oh, just a situation with a dog."
>
> Elissa: "I heard you say you'll be there in half an hour. Where are you going?"
> Me: "Yeah. [long uncomfortable pause] I'm going to go steal a dog with her."
>
> Elissa: "You're gonna what?"
> Me: "I'm meeting her at an abandoned house where a family left their dog tied to a tree."
>
> Elissa: "And then what?"
> Me: [another long pause] "Have I told you lately how much I love you?"

After apologizing for making this decision without her, it was decided that I'd have a family accomplice on this mission: Corey. My youngest son was chosen to drive me to the home where we would grab a dog we knew very little about. It seemed the best option at the time since I don't drive at night because of medication I take for pain. After she agreed to have Corey drive me, I told her of another reason he might be needed.

There was a *slight* chance we might have to break into the house to get the dog. The neighbors had been feeding him and talked about getting him out of the weather. Corey grabbed his coat quicker than Elissa could stop him. There is something about the adventure of helping your dad commit a felony, in this case breaking and entering, that motivates a nineteen-year-old to drop the game controller and move faster than you have ever witnessed.

On the drive there, I explained to Corey what we knew: A retired couple had abandoned their house and moved away. They left their Australian cattle dog tied to a tree in the backyard, and the next-door neighbors had been feeding it. The neighbors called someone who called someone who knew of our rescue organization. Taryn took the call and worked the chain of "notifiers" back to the neighbor who gave her the couple's cell phone number. Taryn got a hold of the husband, who verbally consented to us taking the dog. He explained they simply could not care for it anymore as they ran into hard financial times. A deal was made that we would not report him to animal control if he allowed us to take the dog. He told Taryn the dog's name was Reptar and that he *should be* okay with strangers.

That was it. Corey was now up to speed on everything Taryn and I knew. Well, mostly everything. I did not see the need to explain to my son that there was no way to verify who Taryn actually spoke with. It could have been anyone, for all I knew. The neighbors were so upset when Taryn talked to them, they could have given her any phone number just to see this dog taken care of. The sound of the windshield wipers was the only noise either of us heard the rest of the way there, and I think we both went into that place where you run a bunch of scenarios through your head. Mine included adding up all our bank accounts to see if the sum total equaled the amount I estimated the bail would be if a different neighbor called the New Jersey State Police upon seeing us removing a dog from a house. In the pouring rain. In the dark of night.

We met Taryn in an unlit parking lot directly behind the property. From the parking lot, we had an unobstructed view of the rear of the house. The plan was for Taryn and me to approach the dog. Taryn had a leash in her coat pocket and would hold onto its handle and be responsible for hooking it to Reptar's collar. If he attacked us, Corey was our backup and would use whatever was handy to pry Reptar from either (or both) of us. The three of us, already soaked from the forty-degree pouring rain, approached the yard quietly. We saw the line extending from a large tree but no dog at the other end of it.

There was a shed at the rear property line, and we thought Reptar might be in it. I was nominated to check it out. The sound of rain pelting the shed roof helped mask the sound of my heart pounding. During my twenty-five years as a cop, I had approached a structure like this dozens, if not hundreds, of times, and never did I remember feeling this level of apprehension. Maybe that was because in each one of those previous "tactical approaches," I had a 9mm handgun on my side. And I did not have my child a few feet behind me.

Waiting for a bad guy to lunge at you is what police officers train for. Waiting to see if an angry dog is going to chew you up is not what I was trained for. Lucky for me, the shed was empty. Now the question turned to where the dog could be hiding. As all three of us were checking the rest of the yard, a dog started barking from inside the house. Taryn went to the neighbor's house to see what information she could get, and Corey and I stayed at the back door. The dog inside, presumably Reptar, was barking louder and louder. The barks seemed to be getting more aggressive as if this dog was protecting its property, and we were not welcome.

Taryn was only gone a few minutes before she returned to meet us under the shelter of a small roof covering the back step. She learned that the neighbors were so upset that Reptar was outside in the cold rain they put him inside the abandoned house. They told Taryn that we could go in and get him. They had received permission from the owners. With that information, we pulled on the back door. It was locked. We went around to the front door, and it was locked—time for a different approach.

As Reptar (now confirmed it was him) continued vocalizing his displeasure with our presence, a different neighbor walked over and met us on the front porch. She said Reptar was a nice dog, and she had not ever heard any reports of him biting anyone. Well, that was a bit of good news on an otherwise gloomy situation. The louder Reptar barked, the more outside lights went on up and down the street. We were causing a commotion.

Taryn went around the house to see if any windows were open. Corey stayed with me on the front porch and watched his father jimmy a double-hung window open, a proud moment of handing down an important skill from one generation to the next. By the time Taryn came back around to the porch to tell us we would have to break a window, I had the sashes separated, and we were peering in through an old set of mini blinds that hung at the living room window. From what we could see between the slats, the house was left a mess.

The *breaking* part of this "crime" was committed when I jimmied the window; the only thing left was the *entering* part. Once that was completed, we would have ourselves a full-blown breaking and entering to add to our resumes. The only question was who was going through the window. Taryn looked at me, and I looked at her. Then we both looked over at Corey. He was younger, thinner, and in better shape than either of us. Since he was younger, he was probably quicker too. He knew what we were thinking without us having to say a word. He nodded in agreement and began to reach for the window. Before he could climb in, I grabbed him and reminded him of what he was already taught growing up with dogs.

1. Don't make eye contact with him.
2. Don't make any sudden moves.
3. Take it slowly. There's no time limit.
4. Speak softly, but only if you have to.
5. If he comes at you to attack, give him your arm (dogs will most often go for the closest thing to them when they're attacking).
6. Don't get your face close to his.
7. Stay calm.

He said to me, "Yeah, Dad, I know. Don't worry."

Sure, no worries whatsoever. My flashlight illuminated the room, and we could see Reptar in the hallway, just past the living room. Taryn and I boosted Corey through the open window, and his foot got caught on the blinds as he fell over the couch under the window. So much for no sudden moves. Do you know how hard it is for a father not to laugh at his son falling over a sofa, bringing a set of mini blinds down on top of him?

I yelled through the window for Corey to be careful. So much for speaking softly. I caught myself yelling, so I changed to a whisper, telling him to unlock the back door. What I got in reply was a thumbs-up with his back to me. He was staying focused on a dog that might or might not attack him. Good boy! (Corey, not Reptar).

Taryn and I rushed around back, hoping not to hear any screams coming from inside the house. Corey unlocked the door, and we went in. To our surprise (and relief), Reptar was sitting in the kitchen, and Corey did not seem to have a care in the world. "Look, Dad, he's fine. See, he even lets me pet him." I had hoped Corey wouldn't have gotten that close to his face, but Corey had an instinct and went with it. He tried kindness, and Reptar responded.

I went into the living room and locked the window, then we hooked Reptar up to the leash and walked out the back door as if nothing had happened. But like any hardened criminal knows, time is your enemy, and I still didn't know if we were clear. Someone still could have called the state police, and they might be on their way right then and there. I know response times can vary depending on call volume and manpower. I didn't want to push our luck and try to explain that based on a phone call to an unconfirmed person, we entered a house that was not ours and took something that did not belong to us. I seemed to be the only one concerned about this. Maybe I was simply thinking about how embarrassing it would be, as a retired cop, to convince my brothers and sisters in blue that nothing we used as permission to go and get this dog was able to be confirmed in any way.

I had packed my jacket pockets with dog treats before we left our house. I figured they could be used as a bribe in the car on the way home, a deal between Reptar and me that as long as I fed him, he wouldn't try to eat us. And it worked! Corey drove, and I handed treats back to Reptar, sitting in the back seat. One treat at a time, I was bonding with a dog who was left to fend for himself in an abandoned home. My only worry was that I would run out of treats before we pulled into the driveway.

> "I've seen a look in dogs' eyes, a quickly vanishing look of amazed contempt, and I am convinced that basically dogs think humans are nuts."
> —John Steinbeck

I was hoping the rain would stop before we got home. We still had to assimilate Reptar with the rest of the pack. That involved going for a walk with each dog. We had this routine down to a science by now: the new foster dog would be let out of the car and walked a few houses away. Then, one at a time, the pack members would be taken for a walk with the new foster. This was done so that the meeting of the dogs took place in neutral territory—the street, away from our house. That way, no one felt they had to protect or defend or claim their territory. The meeting was simply two dogs seeing each other for the first time in a place that meant nothing to either one of them.

Bailey was always the first dog of ours to meet the newest fosters. This helped cement her role as pack leader among the dogs. She was alpha and everyone knew it. Even Eiko! She had a way of letting each dog know who the leader was. It never led to a confrontation, and it was as if each dog just knew. If the puppy fosters were playing too rough with each other (in her eyes), she would go over to them and pounce at them while barking. It was her way of saying, "Settle down!"

Unfortunately, the rain kept up, and the temperature stayed in the low forties. Corey took Reptar down the street, and I went in to get Bailey. Being a Lab, she loves water, even if it is rain. The rest of the dogs think she's crazy; they have no desire to go out in the rain. Bailey and Reptar's meeting went great and other than the usual sniffing of each other's butt, we walked at a fast pace so we could get inside and get warm (and dry!). Next up, Eiko and then Rocky. Both seemed to have no problems with Reptar. The only distractions on those walks were more butt-sniffing and a few playful nudges with their snouts. Our other foster, Spirit (a Lab mix), was the most submissive of the dogs we had in our pack at the time. She came out, and she and Reptar seemed to hit it off instantly. No problems whatsoever.

It sounds simple when it's explained that way, doesn't it? To appreciate the amount of time it actually takes, you have to understand how we walk the dogs so there is a lesser chance of aggression. It looks something like this:

(newest foster) (human) (human) (current Williams' Canine Hotel guest)

Notice that there are two people between the dogs on the outside. Each person walking the dog makes sure their dog is to the outside. At first. Once the dogs are walking satisfactorily in that configuration, we switch it to this:

(newest foster) (human) (current Williams' Canine Hotel guest) (human)

This way of walking them is an "every other one" type of situation—human, dog, human, dog. Once that way of walking goes smooth, we switch it again to this:

(human) (newest foster) (current Williams' Canine Hotel guest) (human)

Notice what we did. We put the dogs in the middle and people at either end. This is the real test to see what happens when two dogs that do not know each other are walking side by side. It takes some time to get to this point. First, it's a dog, next to a person, next to another person, and a dog on the other end. Then, it's a dog, next to a person, next to a dog, next to another person. The dogs are getting closer together, but there is still a human between each one. Finally, we get to the point where it's a person, next to a dog, next to a dog, and a person on the other end.

We always end each walk in the front yard to see any reaction to dominance or territorial aggression. But that's not all we do before the new foster dog comes inside; we have to see how the newest member of the pack walks with another dog with just one person. One of us grabs two leashes attached to two dogs. And away we go. This is the final test to ensure there will not be a problem inside. Plus, the structured walk helps cement who is in charge—us humans. It gets the dogs focused on something other than each other.

To figure out how long this takes, multiply everything I just explained by the number of dogs in the house. In this case, in the rain as well. Since I have the most training, I'm usually the one doing that last walk, where one human walks two dogs at a time. Or three. Sometimes four. Once in a while, five, and every so often, six. All simultaneously, together as a pack, walking down the street. Some of our neighbors think we are crazy.

Finally, inside, all the dogs should be tired from the walks, but they are not. They are excited that a new dog made its way into our home. They want to play, and they want to get to know each other. Corey wants to get warm. I want to go to bed. Elissa wants to cook for them. "Not until tomorrow, hun, save it for tomorrow. Please?" And just like that, we were in bed. All of us. In bed. Together. Each dog slept like a baby, and I slept like a dog. In the morning, breakfast time.

> *"If dogs could talk, perhaps we would find it as hard*
> *to get along with them as we do with people."*
> —Karel Capek

And that is when all hell broke loose. Bowls were filled, and water was freshened up. Eiko went to his usual place in the kitchen and waited, Rocky went to his place, and Spirit went to her place. We set a place for Reptar at the other end of the kitchen. Bailey waited right at Elissa's feet as the first to be served. No sooner had all the bowls been put down when Reptar took off toward Eiko. Eiko, who had just started eating, looked up, and I saw the hackles go up as he made eye contact with Reptar. Reptar appeared to be in a trance when he lunged at Eiko, and they went at it. They went at it hard. Elissa instinctively reached down to grab a tail but was unable to. I ran over and grabbed Reptar by the tail and pulled him away from (and off of) Eiko. Elissa stepped between the two and tried to restore calm. I had not gotten up to Reptar's collar with my hand, and his tail slipped out of my hand. He was right back at Eiko. But this time, Elissa was between them.

She screamed, loud enough that I heard it over the brutal barking. When I got to her, Elissa was holding her lower leg in the area of her calf. Her scream startled the two combatants enough that I was able to grab Reptar and put him out the back door. When I went back to Elissa, she was sitting on the floor, holding pressure on her leg. There wasn't a puncture wound, but teeth marks were clearly visible on her leg. She was now running late for work.

I was given the task of repairing the damage in the pack. I worked all day on resocializing the pack, paying particular attention to Reptar. After a few nice walks together, I let Eiko and Reptar out back to see how they responded to running freely without any food to protect (or go after). It took less than five seconds for them to be running and playing together like two best friends. Eiko found a stick and brought it over to Reptar as if to say, "Ya wanna play?" Reptar grabbed one end of it, and they started a playful tug-of-war. But the stick was no match for those two pairs of jaws, and soon the stick was nothing more than a pile of splinters. I had observed enough and decided the rest of the pack should be able to get in on the fun.

The sight of five dogs running free together as a pack is hard to describe. They were all free to be the animals that they were. Bailey was in charge and everyone followed her lead. Wherever she ran, the rest followed; whatever stick she picked up, the other dogs wanted; wherever she peed, they wanted to pee.

Fifteen minutes later, they were all back inside, and their reward was a dog biscuit. Each of them had first to sit, and then they would get their treat. First Bailey, no problem there. Next, Eiko. Again, no problem and Reptar didn't show any interest. Phew! Rocky, Spirit, and Reptar all took their treats calmly, and everything was once again okay. For a little while.

A few hours later, I had the pack resting in the family room, each one claiming a place on the couch or love seat except for Reptar. He decided to lie on the floor in the kitchen with a view of everyone. I turned on the television and sat back to watch a little ESPN programming. I couldn't tell you how long it was, but there came the point in time when all hell broke loose *again*. Eiko was doing nothing but lying on the couch, scanning everyone (including me) as he had always done. His eyes met Reptar's eyes, and that's when Reptar launched from the floor and darted at him. Next thing you know, dog fight, round two. Since I had seen who the aggressor was, I went after him, hoping the non-aggressor wouldn't want to fight.

I grabbed Reptar's collar and yanked him away from Eiko. Eiko looked at me like he was trying to tell me something. I escorted Reptar out the back door and went back to check on Eiko. No blood, just a little bit of fur on the floor. What the hell just happened? What set him off?

Reptar was brought back inside, and I tried something different. This time, I would remove all the other dogs except Reptar and Eiko. Minutes passed, and they were fine; minutes turned to hours, and they were playing together. The other dogs came back in, and everyone got along great. Elissa came home from school and made sure she gave Reptar the same affection she gave the other dogs. There wasn't a grudge held; all was forgiven between Elissa and the dog that left a huge bruise on her leg.

Dinnertime came again, and this time Reptar was fed in another room, cut-off from the rest of the house with a gate. Dinner was served without incident—a glimmer of hope, a step in the right direction. Bedtime came, and the dogs slept together as if they had known each other their entire lives.

Our second full day with Reptar started the same as the first, with the noted exception of where he ate. Elissa was again off to teach impressionable young people web design, computer applications, and graphic design. I was hoping to have a day designed for relaxation. It started great and lasted into the afternoon. It lasted to dinnertime and beyond. It lasted right up until it didn't.

Right around late-night snack time, the fecal matter hit the rotating oscillator ventilator. Once again, all it took was Reptar to make eye contact with another dog, this time Spirit, and it was game on. Spirit didn't know what to do. I knew I had to do something. I jumped in to protect a dog who was way outmatched. In doing so, I got nailed on the arm. It happened when I reached in to separate Reptar from Spirit. I knew I had made a mistake, and I should have reacted the way I was trained.

Instead, I instinctively reached between two dogs going at it. As a result of my stupidity, I got tagged pretty good. Maybe Elissa and I could now compare bruises. Mine would include a few puncture wounds.

This behavior continued regularly until Taryn and I decided to rehome Reptar with another foster family. Maybe a change of environment would help. It was a sad but necessary decision— sad because Reptar was a real lover of the humans in our home, and ninety percent of the time, he was great with the other dogs. But that other ten percent caused havoc and put other creatures in danger.

Reptar went after every dog he ever met. And yet, each of those dogs played with him afterward. Every dog went out back and ran around with him, every dog came back inside and shared a sofa with him, and every dog acted no different toward him after one of the many conflicts.

Elissa came home from work the day she was bitten and made sure Reptar was okay. She wanted to make sure he knew he was still loved. He wasn't treated differently than any other dog. I'm not sure if I could be so forgiving of a dog who left a bruise and swelling that's still noticeable today. I tried, I really tried to be understanding; after all, we didn't know anything about Reptar when we got him. We didn't know his background or his medical history. I tried not to be judgmental, but he hurt my best friend - he injured my bride. It took a lot of work and a lot of thinking, scrutiny of my beliefs and values. In the end, I had no choice but to forgive Reptar.

The next foster family to take Reptar had similar issues, and sadly, one of their children was bitten in a melee involving Reptar and one of their dogs.

Now it was getting to be decision time. As a trustee with the organization, I was involved in very difficult decisions. A trainer on staff with our rescue had been consulted early on in our relationship with Reptar. He had been made aware of each incident and made recommendations each time. Without meeting Reptar, he thought Reptar deserved a chance before making a decision that would be a permanent one. He made room in his home for Reptar and worked with him, one on one, until he believed Reptar was ready to be adopted.

After a few months of being at this trainer's home, Reptar was adopted by a mature couple who had no children and no other pets in the house. Reptar would be an only child type of dog. You should know that he thrived in that home.

"Forget injuries; never forget kindness."
—Confucius

Why did the dogs just "get on with their lives" after each incident? Why didn't they hold a grudge? How could they possibly trust Reptar again? Why was it that Elissa forgave him so quickly for hurting her when I got the cold shoulder for days for buying her a vacuum cleaner for her birthday? She said the one we had wasn't picking up all the dog hair, and she said her life would be so much easier without so much dog hair. What husband wouldn't take that as a hint and go out of his way to make sure his wife's life was easier?

There is a lesson in this story. I'm amazed by the amount of love shown by dogs. I'm embarrassed that sometimes they seem to understand more than we humans. What would you take away as one lesson from the way Reptar was seemingly forgiven by everyone he hurt? Two families had their lives turned upside down, and both not only forgave Reptar each time, but members of each family also went out of their way to work with Reptar in an effort to help him. How many of us would be so forgiving?

And what about Reptar? Is it possible that he's forgiven the family who abandoned him in the first place? Who got the best deal out of this arrangement? Was it Reptar who had his life spared to be given one more chance, or was it each one of us who had been given the opportunity to experience part of his life with him?

Things could have turned out different for Reptar had we given up on him. If the second foster family had not given it their all, Reptar's life would have ended. If an experienced dog trainer had not made room for Reptar and devoted countless hours to rehabilitating him, Reptar would not be with a family who loves him. That family would have been robbed of Reptar's love and devotion. If not for the first act of forgiveness and understanding, and compassion, the love of a dog would have been cut short.

Maybe we can see this dog as a representation of us. Maybe Reptar symbolizes you and me and how we tend to lash out at people from time to time, even people we love and adore. We have all been injured and caused injury, and we have all been pardoned for it. Remember the partial quote I shared at the beginning of this chapter? The one that began, "Life's not the way it's supposed to be. It's the way it is." It was said by the American sociologist Virginia Satir, who is widely regarded as the mother of family therapy. The other half of that quote is, "The way you cope with it is what makes the difference."

We all cope with life differently. It is not always the way it's supposed to be, but that doesn't mean we have to repay injury with more injury. Reptar was pardoned by a number of people, and he received a pardon unlike any you or I have ever thought of. He received a stay of execution. He was given a second chance.

It would seem to me that each one of us has been given a second chance at one time or another; in fact, I bet you can think of a name right now who has forgiven you for something you've done. We have both been pardoned, we have both bitten the hand that feeds us, and that same hand has eventually come back to take ours and share this journey with us. Perhaps that's the lesson. Maybe that is the Good News.

Reptar had Eiko and Rocky as accomplices in this mission
to destroy a roll of toilet paper.

Reptar sitting patiently, waiting for a treat.

4

Where there is doubt, faith
DAKOTA

I am an aviation junkie. I love the idea of flight and all the science that makes it possible. I blame this on my dad. As a young boy growing up in a small town, we learned to find wonder in all kinds of things, and one of them was planes. The Borough of Medford Lakes is a little more than one square mile. Up until a few years ago, it only had one traffic light. Now it has two. It is probably as close as anyone could get to the feeling of growing up in Mayberry RFD. My brother, Glenn, and I were spoiled as kids; we just didn't realize it then.

Our community had (and still has) everything growing boys need—woods, fields, lakes, and one gas station. Nobody locked their doors, and everybody knew one another. Streets were routinely closed for block parties, and a tradition that goes back decades is still going on today, called Canoe Carnival. Floats are built atop two canoes, and they are paddled around the largest lake in the town on the first Saturday night in August.

There is one church, the church where I served as youth minister until I got sick and had to take a medical leave of absence. It's a log cabin church built in the early 1930's. Beautiful stained glass windows let in just enough light to capture the authentic log craftsmanship that was the pride of the builders in that day. What it lacks in energy efficiency (the log walls on the inside are the same logs that make up the facade on the outside— no insulation) it more than makes up for in magnificence. Of all the things I miss since moving to south Florida, at the top of my list is our church.

Through the trees that make up the edge of the Pinelands National Reserve, you could see commercial planes in their patterns going into two airports close to our home. Philadelphia International Airport is a busy airport, and we were lucky enough to have our home right under the pattern for planes that jockey for position to enter the final approach flight path. The other airport is a military post, McGuire Air Force Base. Those military cargo jets are huge! And they fly low, so they don't interfere with the airspace of planes under the air traffic control of Philadelphia. When we were growing up, and every house had an antenna on its roof, we knew when every plane was flying overhead. You know what I'm talking about if you are old enough to remember rabbit ears and directional rooftop television antennas.

If we heard a plane approaching, my dad would take my brother and me out back, and he would ask us to identify the type of aircraft. Was it a 737? Why did we think it was an L10-11? Was it the engine configuration or the tail that gave it away? Being an "airplane spotter" when he was in high school was his way of contributing to the war effort during World War II. A civilian network of airplane spotters helped scan the skies in an effort to thwart any surprise attacks. He joined the Army Air Corps when he graduated high school and would later share his love of airplanes with his two sons.

I miss my dad. He died when I was in my early twenties. My mom died a year before him. They both loved animals and allowed me to have my own dog when I was nineteen, a Siberian husky/shepherd mix named Niko. We had Teddy and Fluffy before Niko, and I cannot remember a time growing up when we didn't have a dog in the house.

Getting back to aviation, I love it so much that I spent thousands of dollars and countless hours on helicopter lessons. I soloed and flew cross country, passed the written test in anticipation of my flight check, and was all ready to take it the following week. And then, I was hospitalized with a possible heart attack. That took care of flying (and the expense that went along with it), but it did not stop my love of aviation. So when the phone rang, and I was told the next transport of foster dogs was coming in by airplane, and the foster families would meet the dogs as they got out of the plane, it didn't matter what kind of dog we were getting. All I knew was that I was going to be able to hang around an airplane that had just landed, and maybe I would be allowed to chat with the pilot. Count me in!

> *"No one appreciates the very special genius of your conversation as the dog does."*
> —Christopher Morley

We were not allowed to drive onto the runway to meet the plane, but we were permitted to walk up to the taxiway and wait. A planeload of dogs was onboard an incoming flight, and all of us foster folks had our eyes trained to the sky in anticipation of more puppy kisses. After about twenty or thirty minutes (what seemed like an hour), I spotted a single-engine plane on a downwind leg, abeam the numbers (of the runway). It was the only plane in the pattern and I knew it was *our plane*. I don't know why I knew it was our plane, we didn't have any communications with it, and this was a small, private airport with no control tower. Perhaps it would be more accurate to say I had a feeling, a strong feeling, that the plane I saw flying parallel to the airport setting up for a final approach was the plane we were all waiting for.

The plane turned onto the base leg, and it looked like a Piper Arrow. Cool! From our vantage point on the apron, I watched the plane bank and descend onto the final approach. He had the numbers in sight, and he was lined up perfectly. His touchdown was just as nice. The pilot turned the plane around at the end of the runway and taxied to where we were standing. After he shut down the engine, he got out of the cockpit and greeted us with a look that said, "They're all yours!"

The pilot, Gary, from an organization called Pilots N Paws, had flown from Maryland in an airplane filled with crates of various sizes. Those crates contained dogs. After the crates were offloaded, they were placed on the apron, and that is when we got our first glimpse of Dakota. Dakota was a black dog, a Lab mix who did not make eye contact with anyone who came near her. Black dogs are the most difficult to get adopted. Check out any shelter, and you will see more black dogs than any other color. The result is sad: black dogs do not get adopted as easily as dogs of other colors, so they get euthanized more easily (and at a greater rate) than any other dog.

Even though Gary flew in from Maryland, that didn't mean that that was where this transport of dogs came from. Pilots N Paws has more than 1,800 pilots volunteering their time. In order to get shelter dogs from one place to another, rescue organizations coordinate with the pilots to get dogs from shelters in distant states to their ultimate foster destination. Sometimes dogs are shuttled from one plane to another during transport, especially if there are a lot of miles (thousands) to travel. In essence, one pilot starts the first leg of the journey and meets another pilot at an airport at a midway point. Then that pilot loads the crates into their plane and continues the second leg of the journey. And so on.

On this occasion, Gary loaded the crates into his plane from a pilot who flew into the airport in Maryland from a southern state where the dogs were in various shelters. A rescue organization in that state coordinated with our organization, so we knew what dogs were coming and hopefully a little background on each one. The folks at Pilots N Paws and pilots like Gary were also involved with that coordinated effort. If you think the cost of gas is high for your car, imagine what the price is at a fuel pump at an airport! So many people, who sometimes literally fly under the cover of darkness, are involved in a transport like this. Most of them donate more than their time. This can get expensive.

If you think your house can get a little stinky when your dog has an accident, think of what happens thousands of feet in the air, with nowhere to go but your destination that could be hours away. Accidents happen, and dogs coming from shelters are scared. They don't know what is going on. They are crated, in a plane, for hours. Any guesses on what the first thing we did when we took hold of Dakota's leash? We found a grassy area and *let her go.* Not let her loose on the runway, I mean *go*, like going to the bathroom, not *go* like saying goodbye.

Let me back up one step, back to the crate sitting on the airport apron with a scared and shivering black Lab mix cowering in the corner. Dakota was a beautiful looking dog—long, soft fur that felt like silk when you touched it. But it would be a while before we would be able to stroke it. It would be a while before we could get her out of her crate. She would not come near the crate's door. Maybe it was because of all the people crowded around, and perhaps it was the strange surrounding—the sights and smells. Whatever it was, she was not coming out. I got a dog biscuit from another foster parent who was there to pick up her newest charge and thought that this would surely work.

Nope. Dakota was not at all interested. The rest of the dogs were already in their new foster parents' cars, waiting to go to their new [temporary] homes. We were standing on a pad of black asphalt looking at a crate with a black dog in it. We were down to one option: go in and get her. Once again, yours truly was nominated to do the dirty work. I think my background of being a canine handler was starting to work against me.

I knew Gary was on a tight schedule to get going. His window (the time frame pilots have to get to a certain place in order to avoid weather or meet certain flight rules) was closing quickly, and he needed to get airborne soon. Here was another dog and another opportunity to crawl through a tight space to get to it. Where was Corey when I needed him? I would be at eye level with a dog I had never met, a dog that was scared to death and acting that way. When you crawl into a crate, there is not much room to turn around and get your face away from the working end of the animal that's facing you. Well, at least we were not committing another felony by this act. I would have preferred a younger, and more able-bodied person take this on instead of a retired, disabled cop.

Since time wasn't on our side, I didn't have time to think. All I could do was look up at Elissa and say, "Wish me luck." Her reply, "You'll be fine. Look how cute she is." Look, I don't know a lot about a lot, but I do know a little bit about a little, and one of the things I know is that not every dog that bites is ugly. Cute dogs have been known to bite from time to time.

I inched my way through the crate door and, on all fours, made my way to within reaching distance of this terrified animal. Slowly, I slipped the leash over her head until its loop was around her neck. And then I stopped. I couldn't help but look at this creature and wonder what had happened to her that made her this sad. I don't know how long I was kneeling there, but Elissa finally spoke up and told me to back out of the crate. Dakota still would not look me in the eye, and she kept her head turned away from me. I've been turned down by women before, lots of women, but this one hurt more than all of them combined.

As Elissa and the rest of the crew saw my best side inching back out of the crate toward them, I kept focused on the dog at the other end of the leash I was holding. I didn't want to turn my back on the girl who would not even look at me. It reminded me of the high school dances I attended as a teenager. Only then I didn't have a leash to work with.

Except for my right hand, every part of my body cleared the crate door. I stopped again, hoping that if she didn't feel crowded in the crate, Dakota would feel safe with me and allow me to gently lead her by the leash out the door. Nope, not a chance. All that happened was that I looked stupid in my position on the pavement—a guy on all fours, barely able to move under the best of circumstances, trying to connect with a dog who had no intention of leaving her abode. However modest it was, Dakota seemed to think that the crate was her home, and she wasn't moving.

Elissa helped me up and took the leash. I don't know what she said in dog language, but whatever it was, it worked. She was able to coax Dakota out of the crate and to her side. Dakota still would not look at anyone, and her tail was tucked between her legs, but at least she was out of the crate. That meant she could empty her bladder (and bowels) on the grassy area alongside the tarmac. It meant Gary could get on his way. Everyone else had left the airport with their new dogs, and I came up with excuse after excuse to hang around to walk Dakota a little longer. By pure coincidence, Dakota appeared to me that she was ready to get in our car just as Gary's plane took off from the runway.

"Teach me how to trust my heart, my mind, my intuition, my inner knowing, the senses of my body. Teach me to trust these things so that I may enter my sacred space and love beyond my fear and thus walk in balance with the passing of each glorious sun."
—Lakota Prayer

Dakota arrived home with us, and we went through the routine of introducing her to the pack. No problems there; she was submissive and disinterested in the other dogs. We then let her run out back with them. Everyone (the ones with four legs) was excited to get out the door and romp in the yard. As soon as the door cracked open a little bit, Eiko used his nose to nudge it open just enough to get his head in there, and then, with his shoulders, he threw it wide open, and all the dogs ran out.

The dogs were running and playing and peeing and pooping—except Dakota. She took herself to an area of the yard behind the shed and laid down. The rest of the pack ran up to her and tried to get her to play, but she wouldn't have any of it. Not knowing if she was sick, we wondered if there could be something seriously wrong with her. Was it more than just the long plane ride?

Elissa and I stood on the deck and watched. Helplessly, we observed a dog introduced to a pack that wanted to accept her, but she appeared to want no part of it. There was nothing we could do but watch from the railing of the deck that every other dog knew like the back of their hand—I mean paw. The deck served as a sort of staging area where the dogs waited to come in and where they hung out and waited, if they were the first out, for the rest of the pack to assemble before racing to the grass in the backyard. It was safe, and it offered comfort and reassurance. It is where we stood with our hearts breaking, watching a dog become a loner instead of a member of a pack of animals that wanted to include her.

After a few minutes, Elissa said she couldn't watch it anymore and went inside to make dinner for the dogs. She called the dogs to go in with her, and their internal clocks knew what that meant— dinnertime! They scrambled through the door, Bailey first, and then the rest squeezed in behind. Now it was just Dakota and me. I did not know what to say or do. More time passed as she wandered in a small arc, always using the shed as a barrier between herself and whatever was in the yard. In this case, me.

There was no trust, no bond of any sort that could be developed like this. Maybe some progress would happen if I showed her I was not there to hurt her, and she didn't come to us to be hurt. Perhaps something positive would happen if I enticed one of her primal instincts: food. I went inside and grabbed a few biscuits out of the jar on the counter. Elissa looked at me like I was crazy. Before I could figure out why I got the look, I saw the dogs, who were all sitting at her feet, run toward me. That is when it hit me. The dogs knew where the biscuits were kept, with the sound of the lid being removed committed to memory. I screwed up the whole dinner routine, and Elissa would be stuck with resetting their attention and dealing with their disappointment in not getting a treat. As I was running back out the door, I looked back and said I was sorry.

Dakota wasn't interested that I had disappeared, no care or worry. When I came back out, she was in the same place she had been when I went in. I walked toward her slowly so as not to spook her. She backed away. I avoided eye contact and acted like I was just taking a walk, not interested in her. She walked away some more. I held out my hand and got down on one knee. If I was holding a ring instead of a biscuit, it would have looked like I was proposing. I thought of calling her to me. There was just one problem with that idea: She did not yet have a name. From the first time we met her to this time of desperation, she was just the dog that we felt sorry for. We called her "poor baby" and "what a shame." But neither was her name; they were feelings we had about her. They described the way we saw her. She arrived to us with no name, and in the confusion and rush of getting her out of the crate, it never occurred to us to name her. Now she was in our backyard, afraid and lonely. She was trusting no one. Not even a guy down on one knee offering a symbol of everlasting love—a dog biscuit.

"Hey, girl, come here. I have a treat for you." It was louder than a whisper but softer than a normal voice. "Here, girl, I got something for you." Nothing. Noda. Zilch. I went from one knee to two knees, and now I looked like I was praying. To be honest, I was. At least I tried. The question was, who should I pray for? Should I pray for the dog in our yard that she would find trust and come to me? Or should I pray for myself that I might discover some kind of wisdom and direction that would help me come up with the right words to get her to come to me?

Dinnertime had come and gone and the light was starting to fade. I stayed on my knees, hoping for divine intervention. It never arrived. Ain't that a kick in the butt when you hope for the Divine to appear? And I waited. And waited some more. Again, nothing; notta, zilch. When doubt creeps in, before you know it, you lose hope. If you are like me, you might even get mad, disappointed again in the lack of God's presence in your life. Have you ever just asked for a simple favor and got nothing for it? Kinda sucks, doesn't it?

"Scratch a dog and you'll find a permanent job."
—Franklin P. Jones

There is a finite time I can stay on my knees. Age and a rare disease do not give me much time down there, if I can get down there at all. If I do manage to get on my knees, I need someone there to help me back up. Elissa was inside cleaning up, and I didn't want to yell for her because the last time I yelled for her from the backyard, she thought I had really injured myself and came running out to save me. It turned out I had just needed help getting out of a chair. I didn't need an ambulance, but she said I almost gave her a heart attack. All the windows were closed, and I knew I would have had to yell really loud to get her attention. That might have given her another close call requiring emergency medical services, so I chose not to ask for her help. Instead, I sat back on my heels and just looked out into the yard.

Sitting on my heels, knees pushed onto the cold ground, I felt as helpless as ever. There was nothing more I could do than roll onto the ground. That is exactly all I could do. I couldn't get up, and I didn't want to call Elissa for help. So I let gravity do its thing and leaned to the side, and there I was, my left ear to the ground, with a view of our backyard that looked different than when viewed from the vertical position.

Lying there gave me a perspective that I had never imagined before. It was probably the closest I had ever gotten to seeing the world from the eyes of a dog. Everything looked bigger, taller to be exact. I decided I might as well just lie there; this decision after assuming all the dog poop had been cleaned up earlier in the day. God, I hope the kids picked it up.

I placed my elbow on the ground and propped the side of my head in my hand, and took in the scenery. Perhaps if I looked like a male model in that pose, Dakota would come to me. After all, who could resist a guy in my shape stretched out on his side wearing the latest fashion trends? After giving up on praying for wisdom and direction, after dismissing the idea that the Divine would intercede and grant Dakota trust, do you want to know what happened? She lifted her head up and looked at me. Her eyes met my eyes, and she stopped, and for the first time since we met, she looked relaxed.

Maybe it *was* the pose I struck. Or maybe she met me at her own level. Whatever it was, it was working. That meant I had a chance. All I needed now was some time to show her I wasn't a threat: no sudden moves, no more eye contact (that might signal I was challenging her), and definitely no loud noises. No sooner did those thoughts enter my brain than Elissa opened the back door and yelled out, "Rusty, where are you?" I looked back at Dakota and saw that she was startled by Elissa's high school teacher voice.

Dakota turned her back to me and put her head back down. Again I heard, "Rusty, where are you?" I didn't want to shout back and ruin all the progress Dakota and I had made, and instead, I whispered. I had my back to the house, so there was not much luck of Elissa hearing me, but I figured I had nothing to lose. She didn't hear me, and the next thing I heard was, "What the hell are you doing laying on the ground?" She had found me after walking out onto the deck and standing by the steps, scanning the backyard for this hunk of a male model. When she saw the sight that could have shocked anyone, she cried out that rhetorical question. It was more than a rhetorical question because more than once, a family member found me in some sort of horizontal position, whether on the floor in one of the rooms in the house or the yard. So I did at least understand her concern.

I tried waving her away with my free arm, silently shooing her away from me. But that didn't work. "What are you doing?" was the next thing I heard. Only this time, it was from directly above me. She had walked down the steps into the yard to see if I was okay. I was. But it was now too late for the connection between Dakota and me; she had wandered off. Elissa told me it had been almost half an hour since she went in to feed the other dogs, and she was getting worried, especially when she looked out the kitchen window and couldn't see me. Elissa reminded me that it was getting dark, and we could not leave this dog outside all night long. Something had to give. I explained to her what had just happened between us and suggested that I might be able to get Dakota to come to me if she went inside. She didn't have a jacket on, and neither did I. I had not planned for this to be a long process when I went out with the dog biscuits some thirty minutes earlier. I suggested that only one of us should risk freezing to death, and since chivalry was not dead in our house, I elected myself to be the one to continue shivering. Elissa gladly agreed and ran back into the house with her arms crossed in front of her, hands grabbing opposite shoulders, mumbling what sounded like "brrr" under her breath.

It was back to just the two of us—Dakota and me. Was she spooked? Did we scare her away, and would I have to wait another thirty minutes for her to trust me again? Thankfully, that answer came relatively quickly. Minutes after Elissa went inside to get warm, Dakota reappeared from behind the shed. But instead of staying where she was before Elissa came out, Dakota continued moving toward me. And not in an unsure way. She held her head up, her tail hanging normally and not tucked up between her legs, and her ears were up. She did not take her eyes off of me. Man, I hoped she didn't all of a sudden feel hungry and see me as an easy meal!

There was nothing I could do if she did see me as human dog food. I was on the ground, and I would stay there until someone in the house came out to help me up. This is where, for Dakota and me, doubt turned to faith. We trusted each other. We knew what the other was (and wasn't) thinking without saying a word. Dakota walked right up and sat down in front of me. Then she did something amazing. She gave me her paw. There, freezing my rear end off on a lump of cold, damp grass, I experienced something magnificent. Sure, a dog giving someone her paw is not exactly newsworthy, but this was more than any dog giving any person a paw. Before this moment in time, this was a terrified creature who did not know what was going on in her world. This moment was about trust. And faith. All I could do was look up and say, "Thank you."

I wanted to share this moment with everyone, but no one was there to see it. I wanted my family to experience what I had just experienced, but it was just Dakota and me. I wanted it to last. So I grabbed her paw lightly. She wanted more. I got a swat from her that she wanted something more than a handshake. She pawed at my hand, pushing it down, away from her arm. My fingers landed right against her chest. That was it. This girl was smart!

For the next couple of minutes, I scratched her chest and belly, but mainly her chest. She seemed to enjoy it there the most. I ran my hand up under her chin a couple of times, just like the dog behavioral specialists suggest when meeting a new dog for the first time. But each time I scratched under her chin, I got the paw. It was as if she was telling me to get busy somewhere else on her body, and the look in her eyes when I reached her chest told me that that was the spot.

I took this opening to take our relationship to the next level, but like on any first date, a guy really never knows if he's moving too fast. Inside my pants pocket was the handful of dog biscuits I had grabbed earlier. Now, if I could just get them out of my pocket. I would need both arms for this: one to hold me up off the ground and the other to reach in and grab them. To give her what I thought she wanted, I would first have to stop doing something I knew she liked.

We are never really quite sure if we should give up something we know is working to risk that which might take us to the next level—in relationships, careers, and life. I found this to be the case as I looked up at a dog who appeared to be content with me petting her for the rest of the night. I rolled to one side, and before I could reach in with my free hand, I got the paw. I tried rolling the other way, using the other arm—the same result. I was afraid if I stopped, she would wander to the back of the yard, and we would have to start over. By this time, my body had begun to absorb the cold and dampness of the ground. I contorted my body in a way that had me reaching straight out with the hand that was scratching and twisting onto my hip so that I could squeeze my free hand into my pocket. And, of course, the biscuits were in that part of the pocket that was still under my body.

Eventually, I was able to retrieve a treat and offer it to Dakota. It would be my second sign of affection, and although it wasn't flowers like most girls would want on a date, I was betting that this girl was different than the rest I ended up on the ground with (in my much younger days), and she would appreciate the gesture. Sure enough, she did. Hesitant at first to take it, she accepted my offer and seemed to enjoy it. I told her that if she liked that, she would love Elissa's cooking. I knew she had been traveling all day, and she had to be famished. Getting up onto my knees, I rolled onto my stomach and pushed up, and rolled back over into a seated position. I was afraid that I might startle her, but she stayed right there in front of me. The second dog biscuit was easier to get to than the first, and she took this one right away. I was making progress. We were bonding. She was beginning to trust me more and more with each passing minute. I sat there and fed her biscuit after biscuit until there was the only one left, not because I thought this was the right way to feed a hungry dog, but because I had no choice. I was stuck there until Elissa came out to help me up. The last biscuit would be used as an emergency treat if the need arose—that is, if Elissa coming outside had scared Dakota, and she ran off.

Lucky for both of us, Elissa's concern for me is both constant and tenacious. I don't get away with much, and when I do get away with something I'm not supposed to be doing, it usually comes back to bite me in the behind, and I end up explaining to her what I did anyway. No sooner had I run out of biscuits (like a guy running out of things to say on a blind date) than Elissa came back outside. This time there was no yelling, no wondering where I was. She knew I had to be in the same spot she had left me. She walked over to us slowly and asked how it was going. I told her me and my date were now getting along great, but it was time for both of us to go inside. Elissa helped me up to my feet, and there, in the last minutes of daylight, Elissa gave her the name Dakota.

Elissa said this dog reminded her of a Native American who'd been displaced by no fault of her own. While she was inside feeding the other dogs and cleaning up after them, she thought of this dog and her travels and decided a Native American name would best suit her. She named her Dakota. Later, we would learn that this name meant "friend" or "ally."

*"Know yourself. Don't accept your dog's admiration
as conclusive evidence that you are wonderful."*
—Ann Landers

I used the last biscuit to persuade Dakota to follow me inside by holding it in my closed hand and coaxing her to follow me. We didn't count on the welcoming committee waiting just inside the back door. Would Dakota see them, get overwhelmed, and run away, or would she see the noses pressed against the glass as friends and allies? Can you imagine being in her shoes? Hungry, cold, scared, and a bunch of folks you never met before clamoring to see you. Are you a starlet or a threat? I saw my first date with Dakota as a success and I wanted to keep it going. So Elissa went in first and corralled the pack in the living room. My date and I then entered the back door together, and her reward for trusting me was the last biscuit; she gently took it from my cold hand. But now, she had to find a way to assimilate with the pack—truth time.

Bailey was let out of the living room first. Some butt-sniffing on her part was the thumbs-up the rest of the pack needed and before long, the rest of the dogs were in the kitchen introducing themselves (a lot more butt sniffing) as a classroom would to a new student. Slowly, Dakota's tail rose to where it was being held high in the air, and instead of being the one chased, she chased a few pack members in a playful way of telling them she could hold her own.

Some three hours after she arrived by plane, Dakota was part of our pack. And to show her just how much she was welcomed in the home, Elissa did what she does best at doggie-dinnertime—she cooked some chicken and added it to a bowl of dog food, and gave it to Dakota. The rest of the pack was kept out of the room as Dakota enjoyed fine dining in a private dining room. It was just her and me. Our date was continuing well, and if history serves me correctly, it was well past a point most of my other dates in life reached. Elissa gave us our time together, and it was nice to see Dakota relaxed and enjoying a meal. Maybe her first meal in a home ever. It's sad when you think of it that way. But I was happy we had bonded, and there was nothing that could come between us now.

Until she was done eating. That's when she left the kitchen to retire to the living room where the others were waiting. Once she got there and saw how they played, she never looked back at me. She was a dog, and they were her equals. I felt bad, but I felt good, if that makes sense. Seeing a dog get along with every member of the pack is a sight that makes you smile. You just want her to be happy. Like seeing my date at the sophomore dance go home with the school's star quarterback—she was happy, and that's what was important.

Let's not overplay the dating analogy. I'm over it more than three decades later. But you know what I'm still not over? All the work I put into getting Dakota to trust me, to trust a human. Who do you think she curled up with when the playing in the living room stopped? If you guessed Elissa sitting in her comfy chair, you would be right! It is a sight to see the energy slowly leave the room as each dog tires out from playing. They all find a spot to claim as theirs once they are too pooped to play any longer. Some head for the sofa, maybe the love seat; one dog might even come up with the crazy idea of their own to lie down on the floor—you know, on a dog bed that's made for them— not a piece of furniture that is made for a human.

Once all the spots were claimed, Dakota looked around and I moved to the side of my chair to make room for her. After all, she had wanted to come sit with me so I could pick up where I left off in the yard—scratching her chest until my arm was tired. All she had to do was climb up, and I would show her how we love dogs in the Williams' Canine Hotel.

She walked right past me…right past me to Elissa, *who was not even looking in her direction.* She put one paw on the chair, then the other. She looked at Elissa, who had her laptop opened, and Elissa looked back at her. The laptop was closed, Elissa's butt shifted over, and the next thing you know, I'm looking at Dakota sharing a chair with my wife. What about the time we spent in the yard? What about the biscuits? What about the moments we shared?

After that first night, Dakota followed Elissa everywhere. She was the first to line up in the hallway every afternoon to wait for Elissa to get home from work, and she was the first to climb in bed with her at night. Dakota found a human she could trust and love in no time at all. A human who trusted and loved her back. And me? I was always her second choice. When Elissa was at work, Dakota snuggled with me. If Elissa was out shopping, Dakota played with me. But when Elissa was home, forget it. Maybe it was the chicken dinners.

Dakota was a dog, and the greatest joy both Elissa and I got was watching her play with the other dogs in the yard. The way she ran made her coat look like it was flowing in the wind behind her. She ran with a stride that was both effortless and elegant. She reminded everyone who saw her of a free spirit. They thought the name, Dakota, fit her perfectly.

Dakota was adopted by a young couple one town away from us. Saying goodbye was tough, one of the hardest up until that time. But we knew she was going to a good home, and our job was never to be her forever home. We were a stayover point in Dakota's life, a place where she would learn how to be a dog with other dogs and how to socialize with humans. It was a leap of faith on both sides.

"I think of life as a good book. The further you get into it, the more it begins to make sense."
—Harold Kushner

What would have happened if Dakota had never warmed up to me? How would her life have turned out if she had not trusted me enough to come over to me and give me her paw? If Elissa and I had not invested countless hours helping her come out of her shell, would she have been adopted?

Sometimes in life, we have to work hard at developing trust, and other times it just happens. Look at me and Dakota and Elissa and Dakota: I had to work hard, and Elissa just let it happen. When we think of faith, do we ever consider that there will be hard work ahead? Someone much wiser than me once said, "Faith by itself, if it has no works, is dead." And while I doubt the reputed author (James 2:14-26) was thinking about fostering dogs when he was credited with this much-used quote (maybe used too much in the wrong context, but that's a sermon for another book), the concept of those words has a way of reminding us that our work is never done.

We can have all the faith in the world in something, but if we do not get off our butts and do something (like reaching into your pocket for a dog biscuit), the very thing we have faith in might just stand there and look at us. And then what? How fulfilling would our lives feel if all we did was lie on the cold ground and wait? It took more than thirty minutes of pleading, coaxing, and calling for a shy dog to even come near me. I cannot imagine what either of our lives would be like right now if Elissa and I had just given up or left Dakota outside.

Think for a moment about the faith Dakota had. Her head had to be filled with emotions like confusion, fear, sadness, loneliness, and maybe even anger. Something inside of her had to motivate her to take that first step. It was Martin Luther King Jr. who said, "Take the first step in faith. You do not need to see the whole staircase, just take the first step."

For me, the Good News here is that doubt doesn't have to be our driving force. With a little bit of work, and sometimes *a lot* of work, we can indeed replace doubt with faith. We can see faith in others instead of doubting their motives; we can see faith in our works instead of doubting our skills; we can have faith in others, and we can have faith in ourselves.

Maybe Dakota can remind all of us that unnamed things in our lives can have a purpose, a purpose that, at the time, is unclear to us. She can remind us that perseverance and determination can put faith back in relationships—relationships that have names like mom or dad, daughter or son, brother or sister, aunt or uncle, niece or nephew, sister or brother. Nameless relationships often become our most precious memories—once we put a name to them.

And when we might have doubts, let's not forget this when we think of perseverance and determination: These two human character traits can be part of the naming of a cherished relationship, namely "friend" or "ally."

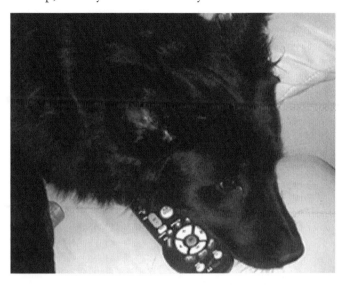

Dakota guarding the channel changer.

The dogs are lined up waiting for Elissa to come home from work.
They did this at the same time every day.

5

Where there is despair, hope
BEAR AND SHADOW

Sometimes the names just come to you. After more than a few successful foster adoptions from our home, Taryn became more comfortable with letting us name the dogs that would be in our care. Remember, there is a real danger in naming the dog yourself. The emotional attachment dramatically increases the risk of you becoming a foster failure, adopting the dog yourself. Every rescue organization has volunteer homes filled with dogs brought in to be fostered but ended up staying in that foster home forever. On the positive side, most rescue organizations wave the adoption fee when that happens.

But this chapter is not about whether or not we would be failures. This is about two Lab mixes that arrived one afternoon. They were brother and sister, and they, along with two other brothers and their pregnant momma, were transported up from another southern state where the euthanasia rate in shelters is extremely high. Not only was this litter of dogs—all less than a year old—going to be killed, so was their pregnant mother. Yes, you read that right. These siblings were less than a year old, and their mother was pregnant again. Puppy mills do not just breed purebred dogs. The back story here is that whoever "owned" the mother didn't want to care for her anymore. Since none of her puppies (the ones in this transport) had been bought, they were thought of as expendable as well. It is amazing what we, as a society, can become when we no longer believe something—even a *living thing*—has value.

These puppies did not sell, and the owner probably thought the still-to-be-born puppies inside this momma were not going to fare any better. So why not dispose of them all? Get a fresh start, clean the slate and start over with a new dog, maybe one that has "cuter" offspring.

I get downright pissed off when I start to think of what happens to living creatures who cannot fend for themselves and, for reasons that are beyond their control, they die. They die because they are killed. We can put a sterile, official-sounding medical term to it like *euthanize*, but the result is the same: These animals are killed. "Sickening" is as close as I can come to describing this feeling.

But for every person who has such a disregard for the value of life, we come across ten more who value life. Maybe the percentages are even higher than that; I will bet less than ten percent of the people we encounter are inherently bad. I will take those odds, and I will focus on the good in people. Are you in this with me?

Are we suckers for trying to see the good in people, or for continuously searching for high morals and true values while overlooking the faults that every one of us has? I guess I—we—could be called worse things for far worse reasons. I am also a sucker for anything that demonstrates honor or valor. I cannot hear *Taps* playing on a bugle without tearing up; I've attended too many police officers' funerals. And *Amazing Grace* on the bagpipes. For the same reason, I become a blubbering idiot as soon as that first note plays. I have also been called a sucker (among other things) for trusting too easily and forgiving too freely. Again, there are worse things a person can be called.

🐾

But what about a dog? What things do we call a dog when they are too trusting or too forgiving? Do we think they are naïve for trusting us? Do we see them as idiots for forgiving us like they do? Any chance they feel foolish when they are deceived by one of us human creatures who share the earth with them?

"Animals share with us the privilege of having a soul."
—Pythagoras

I hope that if dogs do indeed truly forgive, Bear and Shadow forgive me for the two easy puns made after we named them. Shadow was a dog that looked like a Lab mix, a pitch-black coat, longer than that of a Lab, but nonetheless, easily identifiable as being at least part Lab. Her personality was as sweet as any dog that came through our door. And her eyes—her eyes seemed to be able to look at you in a way that had you melting in no time. To a person, everyone who met Shadow remarked at how she looked at them—the beauty in her eyes. Her eyes always followed you, like a shadow. She was named Shadow.

Bear was a large dog. He was larger than Eiko. Bear's eyes were sunken, almost sad. His coat was thick and wavy, with colors of auburn and an orange tone to it that contrasted with the underlying black color. His paws were huge. Bear's ears stood straight up, not floppy like you would expect to see in a Lab. They were triangular-shaped, and they stood up on his head all the time. He reminded us of the *Muppet* character Fozzie Bear. Because of that, we named him Bear.

The puns seemed to write themselves, first Shadow and then Bear. Besides her eyes following everyone as a shadow does, I thought it would be great to tell everyone that I love "seeing my Shadow." Lame, right? Maybe you will understand my pleasure in choosing to give Bear his name. Our backyard is wooded toward the rear of it, and I cannot tell you how much I loved proving an age-old question: A Bear really does "do that" in the woods. Was that second one better? It is the little things in life that make me smile.

The first night in our house involved all the normalcies we had become accustomed to. But their baths were different. They were different not because we changed our routine (no way, we were pros by now), but because of what we found during the baths.

As with most transports, the dogs arrived dirty; some would arrive downright filthy. They all get bathed regardless of how they look (and feel), but when you see the grime and bugs on some of them, you know the bath is a priority when you get them home.

When they arrived as a family of a momma and her four offspring, none of us knew what we were getting. Elissa and I had agreed to take two of the dogs, two other foster families were each taking one of the litter, and another family had agreed to take the pregnant momma. Since we were the first to arrive when the three crates were unloaded, we were given the choice of which dogs we wanted to bring home. The momma was in one crate, and the two other crates each had two siblings. For reasons that are still not clear to me, we chose a crate holding Bear and Shadow.

We took them out of the crates and hooked them up to our leashes. Then they were microchipped and given a quick wipe down with a bunch of those dog wipes because they stunk. They stank, they reeked; they stunk of an odor that none of us had ever smelled before. It was as we were wiping them down that we found what looked like huge ticks on the dogs. Bear and Shadow seemed to have the most of them. We figured we would not try to remove them until we got them home and give them baths so we could really see what we were dealing with. Once they were thoroughly cleaned at our house, we set about the task of removing those weird-looking ticks. There was just one problem: they were not ticks!

Once their fur was pulled away, we could see that what we thought were ticks were actually growths on their skin. Some were small, and some were really big—like heads of cauliflower attached to different body parts. Shadow had maybe eight or ten, and Bear had dozens. His were oozing blood. They looked more than uncomfortable; they looked painful. After recognizing that they were not ticks, it became obvious that we did not recognize them as anything we had ever seen before.

In times like these, you are grateful you have a relationship with your veterinarian where you have exchanged cell phone numbers. Dr. Lori Cobb was our veterinarian, and she and her staff had proven time and again that they were compassionate beyond anyone's expectations And because of that, I was able to take some pictures of these growths and send them to Dr. Cobb. Without seeing Bear and Shadow in the office, Dr. Cobb wasn't able to give a definitive diagnosis based solely on the pictures, but she did alleviate our concerns that Bear and Shadow would be okay until our rescue organization's primary veterinarian could see them. Dr. Cobb suggested that the growths appeared to be caused by the papillomavirus.

The papillomavirus in dogs is relatively benign unless it interferes with eating or the respiratory tract. This is what we learned after doing extensive research the rest of the night, searching and reading every blog we could, reading every article, and looking over dozens of images of the virus. Everything we read and the images we reviewed seemed to confirm what Dr. Cobb told us. The images on the internet sites were almost identical to what we saw on Bear and Shadow. We also learned that there is no cure for this virus. It is treated *symptomatically*— that is, the symptoms are treated to relieve discomfort, but the only treatment to get rid of these growths is time. The rescue organization's primary veterinarian would have to be contacted, and appointments made for Bear and Shadow to be seen.

*"Personally, I would not give a fig for any man's religion
whose horse, cat and dog do not feel its benefits.
Life in any form is our perpetual responsibility."*
—S. Parkes Cadman

Different rescue organizations have different rules about how each foster dog is treated in the foster home. Some organizations ask their foster families to keep the foster dogs separate from human and canine family members. Other organizations ask their foster families to have strict rules about the dogs they are fostering, such as not letting dogs on their furniture and not allowing them to sleep in bed with them. These rules are put into place by rescue organizations for a number of reasons: safety is first, and second is to keep a state of detachment, so adoption is easier (less risk of being a foster failure). Another reason that needs to be mentioned is that when the dog does get adopted, you don't want it to get into trouble as soon as it gets to its forever home because it jumped on the couch or tried to sleep with its new owners.

Elissa and I have heard these rules, and more, from people we have met volunteering with other rescue organizations. We listened to all of them, and after processing what we knew and what we were told, we decided—with the blessings of Taryn—to come up with our own rules. They were as follows:

> Rule #1: Each foster dog that comes into our home will be treated just like any other canine family member.

> Rule #2: Rule #1 shall be enforced at all times.

That's it. Plain and simple. We saw it analogous to being a foster home for children. If we had children of our own and decided to foster another child, how would we treat them? We knew we wouldn't make that child eat at different times than our family. We knew we wouldn't prohibit that child to share in activities that our children enjoyed. We simply could not imagine making that child feel different than the other children in our home. We would hold our children accountable for their behavior, and we would expect them to treat this new member of our household as one of their own family.

We would also make sure we held ourselves accountable. We decided we wouldn't shield any foster dog that came into our home from anyone who decided to visit us. All of our friends and family knew what we had gotten ourselves into, and they also knew what to expect when they walked through our front door. We had hoped that the foster dogs would get used to different people coming and going. When you have two children in college, there is a lot of coming and going with their friends alone. These new dogs came from shelters where they might not have been exposed to humans, other than being fed or having their cages cleaned. We knew they needed to be exposed to as many different situations as possible to feel comfortable around people other than us. They needed to be socialized if they were to have any chance of being adopted.

This was definitely a double-edged sword. Giving puppies freedom can produce interesting results, and it usually does! We never left puppies alone in the home when we were gone. All of them were crate trained. This not only kept them safe while we were gone, it greatly increased the odds of our home looking the same when we returned as when we left. But when we were home, the dogs were able to be dogs. Our home does not look the same because of it.

Every chewed piece of woodwork has a name to it, a memory that will last long after we replace and repaint it. Every stain on the floor has a story to it, and we laugh at them whenever we think of the dog who left us that calling card. Each piece of dog hair, all of them, embedded in our furniture serves to remind us of a love shared—a love shared not only with Elissa and me, but a love shared with our own dogs as well. There is something really special between dogs who share a love that says, "Here, you lie on the sofa tonight."

Yes, our friends think we are nuts. Some of our extended family members cannot believe what we allow. A few friends with other rescue organizations admonish us for screwing up dogs that come into our care. I would agree with the first two statements—we are nuts, and maybe we should have our heads examined. But screwing up the dogs? Neither Elissa nor I can imagine *love* screwing up a living creature.

Three dogs can be fun. Four dogs in the home, and things get really interesting. Five dogs make feeding time challenging. Any more than five dogs, and things can get out of control in a hurry. You can imagine what was going through our heads when we said yes to taking in Bear and Shadow—we already had five dogs in the house! But what were we supposed to do? What do you say when you are told that if these dogs are not pulled from the shelter, they will be put down in less than forty-eight hours?

We said, "What're two more mouths to feed?" When Bear and Shadow arrived, we had seven dogs in our home and two cats. Cats and dogs who did not know each other, dogs of different ages and various backgrounds, all with behaviors and temperaments that kept us up on more than a few nights. And speaking of nights, do you know what it's like to try to sleep with that many dogs in your bed? A queen-size bed is what we have, and two king-size beds are what we need!

"Surround yourself with dreamers and doers, the believers and the thinkers, but most of all surround yourself with those who see greatness within you, even when you don't see it yourself."
—Edmund Lee

Bear and Shadow were now members of our family, and regardless of their skin conditions, they would be allowed wherever the rest of the pack was permitted. That first night, they were welcomed up to our bedroom when it was bedtime. They had crates with blankets in them in the family room, but we made sure to invite them up to bed. Not knowing their background made helping them adjust a little harder, but we never imagined they wouldn't want to come to bed with us. As each light was turned off, making the first floor a little darker with each flick of the switch, Bear and Shadow stayed by their crates. We always left on a dimmed light, and that's how we left them that first night.

As the rest of the pack got settled in and we took turns brushing our teeth, Bear and Shadow stayed downstairs. When we peeked over the balcony that overlooks the family room, we saw that they were in their crates. We didn't know whether to be sad or feel relief that we would only have to contend with five instead of fighting seven dogs for a spot in the bed.

I tossed and turned all night, worried about Bear and Shadow. We had fostered a bunch of dogs by this point, and every one of them wanted to sleep with the rest of the pack in our bed. I was worried something was wrong. Like a first-time father always running in and checking his child in the nursery, I kept getting up and checking on Bear and Shadow. Like most first-time fathers, I finally realized that they were all right.

In the morning, we saw that Shadow had been busy during the night. She had taken all the pillows off the sofas and brought them into her crate. Every pillow on the first floor was in her crate. I don't know what kind of furniture or decorating you like, but I am married to a woman who believes there should be multiple pillows on every available piece of furniture. Don't even get me started with what our bed looks like every night before we get in it. I don't get it. If you are only going to sleep on one pillow—a pillow that is made to be slept with—why do you need ten more piled up on the *real* pillows? Apparently, it looks nice, or so I've been told.

Just as nice looking was the sight of Shadow surrounded by all those pillows. Why do you think she gathered them up during the night? Did they give her security? Could she have liked the way they smelled? After all, I've been told that dogs gather (and chew) things in the house that have the scent of their owners on them. Maybe she was just bored. Whatever the reason, it was darn cute to see that first thing in the morning. Bear, on the other hand, wasn't so cute. He looked like a sad sack. He lifted his head and wagged his tail, but that was it.

Our rescue organization was lucky enough to have a relationship with a veterinarian like we have with Dr. Cobb. By midmorning, we had an appointment with Dr. Keefe, a veterinarian who has helped so many dogs brought into foster care that he knows a lot of us foster families by name. Dr. Keefe confirmed what Dr. Cobb had suspected. He removed one wart from each dog and sent them off to pathology, just to be certain. But there was another reason to lance one growth off of each dog: The papillomavirus is fought off by the body's immune system, and a lot of times, when one growth is removed, the immune system is sent into a kind of overdrive that starts fighting this menacing virus. These growths had deep roots, and there was a hole left in the skin where each was removed. A few staples closed the holes, and we left with a round of antibiotics for Bear and Shadow that would also help.

Days turned into weeks, and there was no change. We thought we saw new growths on both dogs. Shadow had one forming on her lip. Bear's were bleeding more, and we found one in the pad of his front paw. No wonder he seemed sad, no wonder he didn't want to play and romp with the other dogs. Elissa started doing more research on this, and she found supplements that would help boost their immune systems. But this was now at a time when I was going to be in the hospital for a little while, and Bear and Shadow were going to another home, temporarily, until I was back home and on the mend. Selfishly, our focus had turned to me and the upcoming surgery and away from Bear and Shadow.

Mary, another foster in our organization, took Bear and Shadow. It was reassuring to know we could count on someone to help us out when our attention was needed elsewhere. This is one of the wonders of rescue organizations—everyone pitches in when needed. Hopefully, you will agree that this kind of compassion and selflessness demonstrates that we foster folks are not just a bunch of crazy animal lovers who put the needs of pets above our own. Mary demonstrated what happens every day in rescues all across the country. People involved with a cause greater than their own tend to jump in and lend a hand whenever needed—be it a human need or an animal need.

While Mary had Shadow and Bear, she made arrangements with another veterinarian to examine Bear as his growths seemed to be multiplying every day. This doctor felt that Bear's discomfort would worsen if the growths were not removed, and while it would not be a simple surgery, this doctor felt Bear would do well. It took not only this veterinarian, but another one helping him, hours to remove most of the growths that were causing Bear so much discomfort. The surgery was extensive, but Bear recovered nicely, and just about the time I got back on my feet from my visit to the hospital, Bear and Shadow came back to us.

You would think that orders to do nothing for eight weeks would mean having a bunch of dogs around was a bad thing. But I think that it helped me recuperate quicker than I would have in a house with no canine companionship. As I slowly regained strength, so did Bear. Shadow was turning into a real love bug, even though her growths were still visible.

Now, with all of our collective medical procedures behind us, Elissa and I went back in research mode to see more about the supplements that boost the immune systems in dogs. We found a company that sold a powdered product to be added to food. We ran it by our veterinarian, Dr. Cobb, and she was able to research the ingredients in the supplement and believed at the worst it wouldn't harm Bear or Shadow, and at best, it would help them fight off the virus.

A few dollars later, we had the product at our doorstep and began the regiment suggested in the packaging. To be honest, we were hopeful but not confident that this would help. It was simple enough to administer; just sprinkle it into their food bowls twice a day. The hard part was remembering to do it. We didn't expect anything the first week or so. We figured the supplement would take some time building up in their immune systems.

Two weeks, still nothing. Three weeks, nada. But about a month after we started them on the supplement, we noticed Shadow's growths shrinking. The few that were left on Bear dried up and fell off. Shadow's growths took a little while to fall off, but eventually, she was clear of all her growths as well. The transformation we witnessed in both dogs was nothing short of amazing.

Bear not only recovered nicely from his surgery, but he recovered from the sadness that had arrived with him months earlier. He was more alert and willing to take risks when people came over for a visit. When the growths were all over his body, he would stay in his crate and very rarely interact with strangers. While Shadow and the rest of the pack were busy greeting visitors at our front door, Bear stayed back and watched from a distance.

But now that the growths were removed, he played with the other dogs. He even began instigating tugs-of-war in the backyard with whatever stick was handy. Watching Bear romp with the other dogs was one of the most rewarding things Elissa and I witnessed while fostering him and his sister. Being a witness to Shadow developing into a sweet dog who desperately wanted to please others made our hearts melt. And even though she wasn't as reserved as Bear when she still had those ugly warts on her, she came out of her shell in a way that made everyone who met her take notice.

The supplement seemed to work so well on Bear and Shadow that we decided to add it to everyone's food. We figured a boost in the immunity systems of dogs had to have benefits that we didn't fully understand, and it turned out we were right. The coats of the other dogs became softer, and their eyes seemed to light up even more than before. In the end, it proved to be a good decision.

"As anyone who goes into dog rescue knows, it is not a for-profit business, but the rewards are priceless for me."
—Emmylou Harris

Bear and Shadow were our first foster dogs that required medical care. Maybe up until that point, we had been lucky. As mentioned earlier, our organization is extremely fortunate to have a relationship with a veterinarian who could be called anytime, day or night. Dr. Keefe would make room in his day for emergencies that arose. You can imagine if a rescue organization has twenty or so foster homes, there is a constant risk of at least one of those homes having a medical issue. Elissa and I also feel fortunate for the relationship we developed with our personal veterinarian, Dr. Cobb. It certainly gives us a level of comfort to know there is no question or concern too small that she would not answer as soon as she could. We were never made to feel foolish if the concern was a false alarm, and we had nothing to worry about all along. Both Dr. Keefe and Dr. Cobb share an unmatched level of compassion. That compassion carries over to financial compassion as well. Any doctor deserves to be compensated for their time; these doctors give their time to worthwhile groups like ours. Without their understanding of financial constraints, it would be hard to continue.

A few years after we started fostering, I was brought onto the board of directors for our organization. In that capacity, I got to see the bills. The only source of income for this nonprofit rescue was through donations. Whenever a dog came into our rescue in need of medical care, people from all over donated to the cause. Since we decided to pull dogs with medical conditions (dogs that would surely be euthanized due to their illness), bills skyrocketed. The surgery for Bear was higher than any procedure for any dog up to that date. Thousands were needed to cover the cost, which was cut dramatically by the doctors who operated. Their compassion cannot be overstated.

The organization had bills to pay, and we were looking at an invoice that would put us in the red. What is an organization to do? We hit social media, and the result was immediate. Pictures of Bear went up on Facebook and other sites, and before too long, we had donations pouring in. Why does the photo of a suffering dog evoke so many emotions in humans? As a cop, I responded to thousands of calls over my twenty-five-year career, and some were gruesome. During my four years as a paramedic before that, I saw way too much suffering, so much so that I still have night terrors that wake up the entire family. I learned to deal with all that crap, compartmentalizing everything. How about you; what do you do when you witness or experience something that is so horrible you cannot believe it actually happened?

I will bet you and I are a lot alike. You might find the image of a suffering animal almost harder to deal with than human suffering. I don't share that in hopes of you seeing me as callous and hardened so much that I care more about animals than I do about humans. I don't. But there is something about seeing an animal suffering, hurting in ways that we cannot understand because they cannot tell us, which brings me to tears. Maybe that's why requests for donations to help an animal are so successful. Whatever their reasons, people seem to reach deep into their pockets to help a living creature that is in pain.

That was the case with Bear. Thanks to the generosity of people we would never meet, the books were balanced, and the doctors were paid. But none of that would have been possible if not for the kindness of humans—humans showing compassion and mercy. The news is filled with people who do horrible things. Wouldn't it be nice if we heard stories of how strangers help people they do not even know every now and then?

Maybe that is the lesson here. Maybe all we need is the story of a helpless animal in need to stir our emotions to the point where we want to help. Perhaps stories need to be shared of rescue organizations and how they got their start, of families coming together to foster dogs that are about to be discarded, of doctors who demonstrate their love for all of God's creatures, and of individuals who step up and give a hand when one is needed. These stories need to be shared. In doing so, we share the idea that love is a verb. It is not a noun.

We were surprised that Bear was adopted before Shadow. Shadow was so outgoing and lively we thought for sure she would get adopted as soon as all those nasty growths were gone. But a family came to our home after seeing Bear on one of the pet adoption sites where pictures and short bios were posted of every dog in foster homes. They were looking for a laidback dog, and Bear fit the image of what they had in mind. Driving Bear to his forever home was hard. Bear had not been in a car other than driving back and forth to doctor's appointments. What was he thinking? Did he think he was going to get more stuff done to him by one of those people with a stethoscope around their neck?

Thankfully, he did great. As soon as we got out of the car, Bear went right to the front door. We parked in the street, between the family's house and one of their neighbors. There was no way Bear could have known where to go, let alone to the correct front door. It was as if he knew where he was supposed to go, and as sad as it was to see him go, the joy we felt watching him run around the first floor of his new home caused us to laugh. His new family knew how to handle dogs, and he was in the right place. We said our goodbyes and walked out to the car, silent. Corey had come with us for moral support, and it was needed. Elissa and I shared memories of Bear through tears the entire way back home. We were both thankful for witnessing what we had just done and that Corey was willing to take the driving responsibilities.

Shadow stayed with us for months after Bear was adopted. She went to a home with a dog named Jerry—a family who enjoyed the music from The Grateful Dead. This young couple was just what Shadow needed, a family where she could be herself, and they, in return, would give her the love she deserved. The wife of this couple was pregnant when they first met Shadow, and since then, gave birth to a baby boy. We still keep in touch via social media, and the pictures of Shadow and Jerry are like a breath of fresh air, as are the pictures of Shadow with their little boy.

If Bear and Shadow could talk, I wonder if they would tell us if they had any hope in them when they arrived in our home. Covered in grime and thrust into a new home, given multiple baths by people they didn't know, only to find out they had a virus that would cause pain and misery for months to come. What would they have told us of their journey to being adopted? Where did the idea of hope slip in? What would they have told us about ourselves and what we could have done to demonstrate our compassion to others?

There is a verse in the Old Testament that is one of my favorites, and not just for the reason you might think. Let me share the verse, and then I will tell you why it is one of my favorites.

> But the Lord said to Samuel, "Do not look on his appearance or on the height of his stature, because I have rejected him, for the Lord does not see as mortals see; they look on the outward appearance, but the Lord looks on the heart." (1 Samuel 16:7)

This is that part of the Bible where David was going to be anointed king. David was "short in stature." I'm anywhere between five foot five and five foot seven, depending on the colored numbers on the door jambs of whichever convenience store I'm walking out of. So I can identify with the idea of short people doing great things! But look what else is in this passage—

🐾🐾

we're told to look past the physical appearance and see the heart. When I think of what Shadow taught me, I am humbled that a dog is that smart. She saw past my looks and saw my heart; she saw past my physical limitations. Shadow looked past everyone's looks, and she saw their hearts. That's why so many people saw her as a lover, a sweetheart of a dog. Bear demonstrated grace and dignity under the most difficult of times in his young life. People who came into our home initially saw a dog covered with sores and warts. They left in delight, knowing they met a dog with a heart that was bigger than they ever could have imagined. I'm told that that feeling continued long after they left.

It would be easy to say that life is tough, and we need to get used to it, and in doing so, we might find that sense of hope that we all long for. Some people use sayings describing "pulling yourself up by your bootstraps" or "getting over it," whatever *it* is. I don't think it's that easy. I don't think all the despair we witness (and maybe experience) can be replaced so easily with hope. We need someone in our lives to show us hope, to help us find hope. When we hang onto hope, we find ways of climbing out of the hole that we all find ourselves in from time to time.

Look at someone's heart—not their appearance.
Allow others to look at our heart—not our appearance.

Can we do it?

Maybe in the days and weeks ahead, we can help others find hope. We can make a difference in the life of someone we might not even know. We have been shown how to do it, read about it, and now we can be part of it. If we are in need of hope, we know there is someone out there who sees past our defects, who sees beyond our physical appearance. That person sees our heart. You might not realize it right away, but I have faith that every one of us has that someone in our lives.

More Good News, wouldn't you agree?

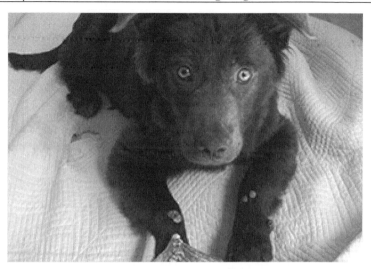

The Papilloma virus is clearly visible on Shadow's paws.

Bear looking sad as he waits for some loving.

6

Where there is darkness, light

ELIOT

When you need someone to lean on, it's reassuring to know there are people out there willing to make sacrifices in their own lives to help make your life easier. That was the case when we needed someone to take Bear and Shadow when I went into the hospital. I can still remember that feeling of relief knowing we didn't have to beg other foster homes to take them. A group message went out to all the foster families, and Mary saw that there was a need, and she stepped up. It was nice knowing we wouldn't have to beg anyone to help us out and that Taryn didn't have to ask another family to take Bear and Shadow.

Every foster family needs to take a break from time to time. You simply run the risk of burnout taking in dog after dog or *dogs* after *dogs* if you agree to take in more than one at a time. We were on one of those breaks, and it was an extended break when Elissa took a call from Taryn. Another family was going on vacation, and they had four foster dogs in their home at the time. For them to get a much-needed two-week holiday, those dogs had to be temporarily rehomed. We try not to put our foster dogs in a kennel except in the most extreme circumstances. If our organization can avoid boarding the dogs in our foster care, we find a way. We make a way. Elissa was asked if we could take two of the dogs.

I learned about this covert phone call later in the afternoon when Taryn called me to find out what time would work to drop off the dogs.

"I'm sorry, Taryn, drop *what* dogs off?"
"Elissa didn't tell you, did she?"
"Hold on, Taryn. I'll be right back."
"Oh, Elissa, I think we need to talk..."

It's hard to be angry at someone when they do something for the right reason, isn't? How could I get angry at Elissa for opening her heart—and our front door—for a fellow foster family in need? It didn't take long to remember the sacrifice Mary made in her home by taking Bear and Shadow. So I just smiled and wondered why Taryn called Elissa and not me.

You women really do stick together, don't you?

Well, our break was officially over when *Eliot* and his brother, *FedX*, were brought to our home by Rob and Jenn, the foster family heading out the following day for Disney World. Eliot and FedX were the last two puppies born into our foster organization. Their momma arrived months earlier, pregnant and ready to deliver any day. Like almost all the other dogs who find their way into rescue organizations, their mom came from a high-kill shelter that would euthanize her, and her belly full of unborn puppies.

Four of their siblings had already been adopted, Eliot and FedX were still waiting for someone to fall in love with and give them their "fur-ever" home. They were twelve weeks old when they ran through our front door. Reportedly they were a hound/shepherd mix, with maybe a little bit of Labrador in them. To us, they just looked adorable, and we could not figure out why they had not been adopted yet. Elissa and I felt relieved that since they came from a loving foster family who took great care of them, they wouldn't need the usual baths that all the other foster dogs that came into our home got. We were off to a good start.

That lasted about an hour before I saw Eliot carrying around one of my slippers. It was one of a pair of slippers that Elissa had just bought for me. They were soft and comfortable. And not cheap. By the time I pried it out of his mouth, the shoelace was chewed to shreds, and the warm, fuzzy lining was chewed and soaked with slobber. No sooner did I put that away than Elissa found FedX gnawing on the kitchen's center island. Bailey and the other dogs just looked on from a distance as if to say, "What did you expect was going to happen?"

Personally, I think our dogs could have stepped in and given us a hand. Maybe they could have barked? Something to get our attention? Nope, all they were concerned with was playing with the puppies in the backyard. And out they all went! We had forgotten just how quickly things could turn from calm and serene to all hell breaking loose. While the pack was outside burning off some of their energy, Elissa and I went around the house in an attempt to puppy-proof it as much as possible. After we were satisfied we had done all we could do, we let them in and gave our dogs a chance to teach Eliot and FedX how things worked at the Williams' Canine Hotel.

Our dogs all sat in a line in front of the counter where the dog biscuits were kept. No one got anything until everyone was sitting calmly. At first, Eliot and FedX did not know what to make of this weird ritual. But as soon as they saw each dog getting a treat, they knew something good happens when they sit. It took a little while, as well as a lot of patience, but Elissa finally got both Eliot and FedX to sit—not at the same time (that would come later, much later), but they did sit. When they sat, they received a nice little reward.

Phase one of establishing who is in control and the concept of reward training was now complete. We could move on to phase two, making it clear which dog was in charge of maintaining foster dog decorum. That would be Bailey, and again, as with every other foster dog that came into our home, she did it without showing any aggression or dominance, and somehow each and every dog knew what her role was.

"Whoever said 'Let sleeping dogs lie' did not sleep with dogs."
—Unknown

By this point, we were thinking that things were not going that bad at all! Next up after playtime would be bedtime. I've got to say, it was really nice having to share a bed with *only* three dogs for the time we were on hiatus from fostering. Eliot and FedX shared a large crate at their previous foster home, and that crate was delivered with them. We were told they sleep in it together and there shouldn't be a problem. The crate was in the family room, and our bedroom was on the second floor. We ushered them into the crate and said goodnight. Then we went upstairs to go to bed—Elissa, me, and the other foster dogs. The cats were already there waiting for us.

After I found my sliver of the edge of the mattress, Elissa grabbed whatever blanket she could and tried to cover her shoulders on the other edge of the bed. The dogs had the middle to themselves. No sooner had the lights gone out than Elissa asked me, in a whispered voice, if I thought the puppies would be okay. I reassured her that they were.

"But what if something happens? We won't hear it."

"Hun, they're fine. I promise they're going to be fine. Go to sleep."

"But don't you think it's unfair that our dogs are up here and Eliot and FedX have to stay downstairs?"

"Seriously?"

"I'm serious. I don't think it's fair at all."

"What do you want me to do?"

"Don't you think they should be up here with us?"
"What do you want me to do?"

"I'm asking you, don't you think they should be upstairs with all of us? Don't you think it's unfair?"
"If you think it's unfair, then I think it's unfair. Let me go get their crate and bring it up here."

"But you...you don't think they should sleep with us?"
"Where?"

"In bed. In bed with everyone else."
"Sure. Why not..."

Three dogs, two cats, and two new puppies later, and we were all set for a good night's sleep. Even though we were now set for a good night's sleep, that didn't mean that it actually happened. That's because our newest fosters thought being on the bed was really cool, and they wanted to play. They wanted to play with the dogs. They wanted to play with the cats. They wanted to play with Elissa. They wanted to play with me.

Being exhausted after that first night does not come close to describing how my body felt. Five bowls needed to be filled instead of three, and it was only seven o'clock in the morning. Oh, how much I'd forgotten.

Within two weeks, an adoption application had come in for FedX. We had blasted their photos all over Facebook, and one of Corey's friends saw them. He wanted to come over and see FedX, so he completed the online application, and once that was approved, he came over. Rob stayed more than two hours playing with FedX and Eliot, learning everything he could about them. Although Elissa and I tried to convince him to take both puppies, the rules of his apartment complex permitted only one dog. He really hit it off with FedX. Corey and I drove to Rob's house with FedX in the back seat two days later.

Eliot was now the last puppy in the litter who still had not been adopted. I don't know if he was the runt of the litter, but he certainly was not the alpha dog. When he and FedX played, he was always the one being dominated. Their play got rougher as the weeks went on. It got so rough that there were times Eliot cried out in pain; FedX was biting him that hard. When they arrived at our house, we noticed Eliot had scabs on his neck and back. As we watched the way they played, it became obvious that FedX played to win, and he would bite Eliot on the back and hold him down by his neck. This went on all day, every day. For as long as FedX (who was a sweet dog with a great disposition) was in our home, he took charge of Eliot. We wondered again if Eliot was the runt of the litter.

> *"Rambunctious, rumbustious, delinquent dogs*
> *become angelic when sitting."*
> —Dr. Ian Dunbar

With FedX gone, Eliot was able to be himself. He no longer had to worry about his brother jumping on him, ambushing him around every corner. Eliot could just be Eliot and play with the other dogs who were not there to dominate him or cause any problems. Yep, no problems for Eliot to deal with. Do you know why? Because Eliot found enough problems on his own:

- Another pair of slippers—well, just one of them, but it was the same foot as the first pair, so I was still screwed.
- Baseboard moldings.
- Staircase treads (the nosing—that curved part hanging over each riser).
- Cord to my electric shaver.
- Cord to the vacuum cleaner.
- Cord to a videogame system.
- Videogame controller.
- One of Elissa's paintings.
- Elissa's sneakers.

- Two cell phone chargers.
- Corey's wallet.
- Railing on the deck.
- Screwdriver.
- Computer power cord (to *my* laptop!).
- A bunch of other things I've allowed myself to forget.

Eliot was curious. He was cute, adorable, loveable . . . and curious. He was curious about *everything*! And it was that curiosity that made him so much fun to be around. Did you ever watch a puppy go outside? Everything is new to them. It's like when Eliot went outside, he was experiencing it all for the first time. Every time. Just watching him follow a leaf falling to the ground—he was in awe of it. He chased it and tried to grab it out of the air. When he missed on the first try, he didn't give up, and he went right back after it. Wind be damned, he was determined to get this thing that fell from the sky.

I have been accused of waking up in the same mood every day. I wake up, and I'm happy. If I wake up and my feet hit the floor, that day is Thanksgiving. When you wake up with "an attitude of gratitude," the day seems to go your way. Are there days that I do not feel that great? Sure! But just because a part of the day, the beginning, is not great, that doesn't mean I cannot look forward to the possibilities of what the rest of the day will bring. Does it sound crazy? Maybe, but I think we all have a responsibility to others around us, especially our friends and loved ones. We cannot promise to feel a certain way, but we can promise to act a certain way.

Waking up to Eliot licking my face is something I miss to this day. He would wake up, and his tail would be wagging. Just like that, he was awake, and he was happy about it. Elissa and I were happier than him if we could get him outside before he had an accident on the floor!

Eliot would run around with the other dogs, and you could see how excited they all were to be outside. They looked forward to just being outside. Eliot didn't stop his good-natured fun when he came back inside. That fun (and curiosity) continued all day long. It was amazing. Dogs wake up in the same mood every day, a great mood. They expect that the day is going to be a good one; they have no thoughts of anything but what this particular day has to offer. It seems we can learn a lot from dogs.

If we can learn from dogs, can dogs learn from us? God, I hope so. If you've ever watched a dog, you soon realize that they learn a lot from their environment, and if that environment has cats in it, you can bet that a dog will learn from them. Eliot was no exception.

When he and FedX first saw Bellagio and Bojangles, they had no idea what to make of these strange creatures. Our two cats didn't take long to demonstrate why felines rule the wild animal kingdom. Before I go any further, you need to know that both cats have no front claws; they are both inside cats. And no puppies were harmed.

As stated in an earlier chapter, Bellagio and Bojangles became experts in determining just how close they could get to any new dog in our house, and they knew every escape route by heart. Almost every one of those escape routes included using height to their advantage. They would simply jump on something higher than the dogs could reach. This might be a piece of furniture, a counter, and in some extreme situations, the top of our kitchen cabinets. But when the situation was more a nuisance in their mind, they would stand on a counter or piece of furniture and then beat the living snot out of the dog's face with their paws. It looked like a lopsided boxing match, the kind where the opponent doesn't know whether to bob or weave.

And again, since they were declawed, there was never any injury to any of the dogs. It was just entertainment for us to watch. FedX and Eliot soon learned that by chasing the cats, they had playmates for as long as they wanted their snouts smacked because the cats never got tired of letting them know who was in charge. The advantage became even more obvious after FedX was adopted. Now, not only was it a feline power play, but it was two against one—Bellagio and Bojangles against Eliot. I have to hand it to the little guy. Eliot was not one to give up when faced with insurmountable odds. He pressed on, but he kept leading with his nose instead of how I tried to teach him. A polished fighter *never* leads with his nose.

The cats, especially Bojangles, taught Eliot one more thing that proved challenging for him. They taught him how to leap from object to object. Whether from dresser to dresser, counter to counter, or sofa to newel post, Eliot witnessed just how far cats can leap. He got to see their amazing vertical leap as well.

This was all new to Eliot, who never saw a cat in his young life until he lived in our home. I would imagine it looked like fun— leaping across the kitchen floor instead of walking on it, jumping to and from different pieces of bedroom furniture, and somehow sticking the landing on that post at the top of the stairs. I can only guess how many things were going through his head, but I am sure he saw this as a challenge. Eliot was rapidly showing us he wasn't one to back down from a challenge.

Our first glimpse of his determination to be like a cat was watching television one evening. Elissa and I were relaxing in our chairs, and the dogs were resting on whatever piece of furniture was available to them. Eliot was on the love seat when he must have seen an antler on the ottoman that Bailey left behind. Without any warning, Eliot leaped from the love seat and landed on the ottoman, about four feet away from the sofa. We could not believe what we had just seen! But this would be just the start of things to come.

The more Eliot chased Bojangles on the counters in the kitchen, the more Bojangles jumped over his head, going from one part of the kitchen to the other. Eliot stood there watching a cat seemingly flying in the air right over his head. Eliot jumped up and tried to do the same. It did not work nearly as well as it had for the cat.

We now were watching a cat flying through the air in the kitchen, launching over a puppy who was on his hind legs trying to get airborne. And then, said puppy would do his own thing in the living room and family room—launching from one couch to another, running full speed onto a sofa, and with that momentum, he would jump across the room onto another piece of furniture. He never seemed to tire of this, but the other dogs did. And Bailey, being the canine enforcer in the home, would run up to him and bark. We assume this was in an attempt to get him to stop. Her barks fell on deaf ears as Eliot continued this indoor gym play until Elissa or I stopped him. It wasn't that we didn't enjoy watching it; we were afraid he would hurt himself if he missed one of his intended targets.

> *"Even after all this time the sun never says to the earth,*
> *'You owe me.' Look what happens with a love like*
> *that. It lights the whole sky."*
> —Hafiz

What was supposed to be a few short weeks turned into months and months of trying to get Eliot adopted. There was a lot of interest, but no one pulled the trigger and completed an adoption application on him. This created more than one problem, the first being we were really starting to fall for this guy. He grew in our hearts as he continued to grow in size. Unless you want a house full of your own family dogs, this can be a dangerous thing. The other problem was that he was getting accustomed to our way of doing things. This could make it harder for him to get used to doing things the way his new (future) family operated. That can lead to confusion and behavioral problems if one is not careful. Our concern was not without merit.

When a dog becomes part of your family, as all our foster dogs did, certain changes take place in your heart. One is acceptance. Another change that happens is the slow melting of your heart. These changes are amplified when you are not feeling well. I don't know what you think of coincidences, but I tend to see them in what has become a fairly well-known quote attributed to Albert Einstein: "Coincidence is God's way of remaining anonymous." I'm not asking you to agree with this statement or agree with anything for that matter. I believe having an open mind is more important than thinking we're right. But just for a moment, think about how it must feel when you are feeling lousy, and a dog arrives that seems to be able to sense your aches and pains. That is what happened with Eliot and me. It was because of a whole lot of aches and pains in this old body that Elissa and I took a break from fostering. When Eliot arrived at our home, the last thing I thought I needed was another dog to take care of, or another thing that Elissa needed to take care of, in addition to her other responsibilities *and the stress* of dealing with everything she had going on with me.

Either this was an amazing coincidence, or something was going on that I did not know about. Either way, Eliot helped me in ways he could never have imagined. Nor could any of us who had been a part of his young life up until this point. I'm in pain, not just some of the time. I'm in pain *all* of the time. The only variable is the number (as doctors like to scale it) of my pain level. Medications and operations to implant devices in me help, but nothing completely takes away the pain I'm in.

While Eliot didn't take away my pain, he did give me a break from it. Eliot was the distraction I needed at the very time I needed it the most. Since my diagnosis, my back pain has been getting gradually worse. The increase in pain (and conversely, the decline in my quality of life) couldn't be measured in days, weeks, or even months. It had to be measured year by year. If I were to look back at each passing week, I wouldn't be able to evaluate how much the pain increased. I could only say that I was in less pain this time last year. That type of evaluation has continued for me to this day.

The summer Eliot arrived in our home was different. The pain was getting worse on a regular basis. My quality of life was decreasing in a measurable way that I had not been able to see before that summer. That is why I thought the last thing we needed was a new puppy in the house. I soon learned how wrong I was.

We were on high alert from the minute he and his brother arrived. There wasn't a moment we couldn't take our minds off what he and his brother were doing. We were constantly thinking of what we had to do next, of what we had to "Eliot-proof" next. When I say constantly, I mean *constantly*. When we failed to keep our minds going, Eliot certainly had a way of reminding us. A simple review of the bulleted list a few pages back should give you an idea of how he reminded us!

When he wasn't sleeping, we were busy. It was almost like having a baby where your sleep schedule revolved around theirs. You slept when they slept. Chasing a puppy around all day, every day, will certainly give you something to think about other than your own problems. That's for sure. But Eliot did more than cause enough problems that neither one of us (or our kids) got any rest, he discovered a way to help me feel better by snuggling next to me when I felt like crap. Eliot seemed to have a built-in barometer of sorts that sensed when my pain level was up; when I was in pain, he was next to me. Not on the floor next to me. He was *next to me,* like sharing the chair next to me.

There is a reason most hospitals have programs that allow therapy dogs into patients' rooms. Dogs have a way of not only breaking down barriers, but building up people in the process. They have an uncanny ability to turn a dark day into something meaningful. When we think of something positive, it's difficult to feel something negative. Go ahead, give it a try. Think of a memory that makes you happy. Now remember that and try to feel down. Sure, you might be able to feel down immediately after that thought from your past, but in that moment, you couldn't feel down. It is just the way our brains are wired. The reverse is also true. Try to think of something that's sad, something that brought misery to your life. I will bet you did not (or could not) smile when you were thinking of that. We become what we think. At least, I'm pretty sure of that.

If you know someone who is experiencing chronic pain, you know what their day consists of. It revolves around pain. Whether it is a lot of pain where you cannot do anything, a little bit of pain where you are able to get things done, or hoping you don't have excruciating pain later when you want to do something. Everything revolves around pain. It's more than just a distraction when your day is able to revolve around something other than pain. Something that gives your life a sense of worth—to be needed—is much more than a distraction. It is a lifesaver!

With Eliot next to me, I felt needed, probably because he needed someone to pet him, and he let me know it. Instead of feeling sorry for myself, I felt useful. I was needed. At least my fingers were needed. When the momentum of Eliot's weight caused the furniture to move when he leaped from one piece to another, I was needed to nudge them back to their original spots. I figured Eliot had the jumps measured to the inch, and I didn't want to see him miss, so I would walk around the rooms he just left, nudging sofas and ottomans back to where they were before Eliot started his routine.

And of course, Eliot needed someone to feed him and give him his treats, and Elissa was kind enough to allow me to assist her in this task. There is a deep bond created when you feed another creature, isn't there? When someone or something is dependent on you, the relationship is either strengthened or weakened. It becomes weakened when score is kept, when we think who owes who on a quid-pro-quo basis. It never balances out, does it? But magical things happen when we stop keeping score and understand our dependence on one another.

Eliot never felt (as far as I know) like he was mooching a free meal off of me. He understood that I—and every one of us— was there to take care of him, to give him shelter and food. I didn't feed him hoping to get something in return, and I didn't hold him accountable for anything in return for me feeding him. I needed to understand what my role was as well. In life, those roles can change at a moment's notice, and often do. One minute we are the one who is doing the feeding (taking care of another), and the next thing we know, we find ourselves in a situation where we are the ones needing to be fed. We are dependent on one another.

Going into that summer, I never would have guessed things would go downhill so quickly. I never thought there would be days as dark as the ones that led up to Eliot coming into our lives. I could never have guessed that a puppy, filled with more energy than all the dogs in our house at that time, would bring me out of that darkness. It is unimaginable that a dog can make you forget about what is bothering you or how much pain you are in. Or is it?

In his book, *Being Mortal,* Dr. Atul Gawande notes different studies that demonstrate how patients thrive when they have something to take care of, be it a plant, a bird, a cat, or a dog. He recounts an interview with a nursing home director who allowed all these into his facility. Then, two years after this groundbreaking idea, the effects were studied. Researchers compared the quality of life with another nursing home in the area, and the results were astounding. Prescription requirements were half of the control nursing home. Psychotropic drugs for agitation were down considerably. Total drug costs were just thirty-eight percent of the comparison facility, and deaths fell by fifteen percent.

In short, when people have a purpose to live, they live not just longer, but better. In some cases, *much* better. It is so obvious it makes you go, "Duh!" And yet, we find ourselves repeatedly amazed at how much pets contribute to our lives as if we're surprised. At least that was the case with me. Having grown up with pets all my life and worked with dogs for more than three decades, I should have known this. I wondered if I had begun to take so much for granted.

When we get in that dark place, it can be hard to see any light. If we do see light, often we're seduced into not trusting it. We look for reasons to doubt it instead of reaching for it. And then, seemingly out of nowhere, something (occasionally with four legs) gets dropped right into our laps. If we're lucky, that thing cuddles in our laps once it arrives.

It makes you wonder, doesn't it? If something as innocent as a helpless puppy can bring light into our lives, what else is possible? What else, or who else, can bring light into our lives? Where could we look to find it? When you think about it, the possibilities are endless!

Eliot taught me that there are always reasons to, quoting Monty Python, "Always look on the bright side of life." His love for life was infectious, his curiosity contagious, and yet his looks were benign. There was nothing about his looks that made you think he was the best-looking or the ugliest dog—just an average-looking pup with a huge heart, the kind of mutt that melts your heart.

When I think of the times my heart's been melted, I cannot help but remember it was because something, or someone, gave me a reason to think about them and not me. Maybe when we think of someone other than ourselves, we open our hearts to seeing a light that shines where before we saw nothing. I doubt I am the only one who has seen something special in someone, but when I mentioned it to them, they shunned the idea and replied that they didn't see anything special in themselves. What about us, you and me?

Have you ever had someone tell you they saw something special in you, but you rejected it outright?

Perhaps you and I can continue this journey by understanding that when we shine a light on others, we light up their lives in ways we could never imagine. We put light where darkness once lived in their hearts. When we have an opportunity to help another living creature that is dependent on us, may we always think of puppies like Eliot, who unknowingly shone a light where darkness once lived. It's a reminder of the Good News that bounds from sofa to chair to the kitchen counter, a joy that shines a light in your life and in mine.

Eliot enjoys the furniture as much as – or more than –
his human foster parents.

7

Where there is sadness, joy
ROSIE

"Once upon a time, there was a princess who..."
"Once upon a time in a faraway land, there was a tiny kingdom..."
"Once upon a time, there lived a..."
"And they lived happily ever after!"

According to the Oxford English Dictionary, the stock phrase "Once upon a time" has been used at least 1,380 times in (English language) storytelling. We all know how these stories end. More often than not, the fairy tales we have heard since childhood end with, "And they lived happily ever after."

That happens only in fairy tales, right? I mean, in real life, the ugly duckling doesn't see herself as a beautiful swan in the end. Most of the time, the ugly ducklings in our life remain ugly ducklings; be they the homeless, the lost, the addict, the unwed mother, the bastard child, the immigrant, the depressed, or the physically deformed. There's a national headline of a ninety-year-old man and two ministers being arrested in Fort Lauderdale, Florida, for violating a city ordinance by feeding the homeless.

We tend to find ways to push the "ugly" out of our sight at almost any cost.

This is a straightforward story of a dog named Rosie. This is a true story. It's not a childhood fairy tale written by Hans Christian Andersen. This is her story. And it is our story.

Here's the blog, written by Rosie's human adopter, Ginny, the night she brought Rosie home from our house:

> Pretty Is, As Pretty Does!
>
> Beauty is not in the face; beauty is a light in the heart— so said Kahlil Gibran. See...all my life I've sought the beautiful— in music, in art, in photography, in objects to paint. Which doesn't mean that everyone else has to agree with me—but at least I found these things aesthetically lovely.
>
> To my mind there is no more beautiful dog than a golden retriever. The sight of a golden standing in the wind with fur and feathers blowing just grabs my heart. I've been fortunate in having two beautiful Golden Retrievers. My first, Hannah, lived to 12, and my current Golden, Miriam Rose, is 13 1/4. I had promised myself when Miriam died, I would adopt a shelter dog, but I had some strong preferences. I wanted a large dog with soft fluffy fur, with some of the Golden loveliness in her. But I imagine the Divine mind had something else planned— a life lesson to be learned.
>
> I brought home last night a shelter dog who had been in a wonderful foster home. She came from a high kill-shelter, and was the only one not going to be transported north for adoption. She heralded her arrival to my house by nervously leaving a trail of pee through three rooms! Rosie is her current name, and no one was rushing to adopt her because she is 2 yrs. old, and because she will never win a beauty contest. She has a corgi body—white

with brown blotches, freckled bowed legs, an optical problem called *cherry eye* in one eye, and her lower jaw is thrust out so her lower teeth jut out as well. She couldn't be any more opposite from what I envisioned! But she is a gentle, loving little girl—and after a while, you begin to see her as beautiful. A wonderful example of the old adage, "You cannot judge a book by its cover."

This is not the first time I've been treated to God's particular brand of humor! Fortunately, I can laugh right along! Things are not definite yet since we're trying this out to see if the two dogs can get along. But I suspect that the dapper Rosie has found a new home.

And they lived happily ever after.

Right? I can report that Rosie did indeed stay at that home. She was adopted by a wonderful woman who is dear to our hearts.

Every great ending has to have a beginning. Now that we know how it ends, let's go back to the beginning. This is the story of how it all started, of how they lived happily ever after.

Elissa and I were notified of an upcoming transport where our rescue organization would be pulling dogs from more than one shelter in a southern state where the euthanasia rate was among the highest in the country. Time was of the essence, and the shelters were not just taking a verbal commitment to spare the dogs' lives. They were going to euthanize these animals on a certain date at a certain time regardless of any promises by rescue groups to pull them.

Most of the time, rescue organizations get *urgent euth lists.* These are lists from shelters across the country that publish the names and brief descriptions of dogs scheduled to be euthanized. These descriptions include the breed (if not known, what the dog is believed or appears to be), age, temperament, health, any behavior issues, and a history of human aggression or bites. A picture is included in each description.

Taryn called me at home while Elissa was at work and told me that all of the dogs that our organization was pulling had foster homes ready for them. There was just one issue that Taryn wanted to run by me. One of the shelters we were pulling from advised her that all but one of the dogs on their euth list were being sent to various rescue groups. Just one dog was going to be put down. All the other dogs had rescue organizations coming for them. When Taryn heard this, she called me.

What was I supposed to say, especially after she emailed me a picture of *the one dog* that was going to be put to sleep in a few days? The only issues we could think of why this one dog didn't get pulled by any other rescue were her age and her looks. Those are two biggies. There was no mention of any behavior issues. This dog was said to be very friendly—nothing about dog or human aggression and no major health issues. The only health issue was what is called a *cherry eye*. A cherry eye is a bulging of a tear duct in the corner of the eye. It looks painful (and weird) but is not considered life-threatening and is painless in most dogs. The other issue was her age—older dogs have a harder time being adopted, and this dog was more than two years old.

> "Love does not consist of gazing at each other, but looking outward together in the same direction."
> —Antoine de Saint-Exupery

I ask you, knowing all that I have already shared, in addition to a photo of this dog tugging at my heart, what was I supposed to say? I said yes and sent Elissa an email to her work, explaining the situation and asking her to understand. I followed that up with a second email with the photo of Rosie attached. Almost immediately, I received a reply from Elissa. She thought Rosie looked adorable and didn't care about her age (which could mean an extended foster period). She told me I had made the right decision. Yes, a wife told her husband he made the right decision!

I was tempted to note the date and time—just in case I needed it for future evidence.

I was never worried. We were a team and still are. As long as a decision is made out of love, we support that decision. Phew, thank God!

Of all the dogs we fostered up to that point, this one felt *the most right.* It was always good to know that we were saving dogs and that we were part of an organization committed to doing the same. But we never had an opportunity to take the one dog out of an entire shelter that would be killed if *we* didn't take it. That was a lot to digest. I have to admit, it was almost too overwhelming to think about. An entire shelter would be cleared out of all the dogs who were scheduled to be put down, except for one dog. I cannot imagine what it must have felt like for Rosie if she was aware of what was going on. Could you put yourself in her position? What would that feel like if you knew you were the only dog not wanted? And on top of that, because you were not wanted, you were going to be put to sleep. It makes you think, doesn't it?

Rosie arrived well after dinnertime since the transport vehicles were changed twice on the way up to New Jersey. The first caravan brought them part of the way, then the next caravan picked them up and took them to a staging point north of us where our organization and other rescues took their preassigned dogs and brought them to their respective locations. By the time Rosie and the other dogs coming into our rescue arrived, it was past seven o'clock. We were sure she had not eaten, so Elissa cooked up her special "welcome to our home" canine meal for her. Rosie ignored the other dogs as she enjoyed her first meal in presumably an entire day.

As hard as it is to admit, I was a little disgusted when I first saw Rosie. It was that thing on her eye. It looked like it was so uncomfortable, and all I could think of was how that would feel if it was in *my* eye. In my four years as a paramedic and twenty-five as a police officer, I witnessed my fair share of trauma. Trauma calls were the most challenging for me, and I enjoyed that challenge as both a paramedic and a cop. But the one type of trauma that I never got used to, the one kind of call that made my knees weak, was eye injuries. I could see a lot of sick stuff, but something in the eye, and I was almost worthless to my partner. I think it came from an incident during my childhood when my brother aimed an air rifle at me and pulled the trigger. Before he pointed it at me, he shoved it in the ground, and a plug of dirt was lodged in the end of the barrel. When he pulled the trigger, the glob of moist dirt struck me right in the eye. I didn't know what pain was until that moment in my young life. Ever since then, nothing could go near my eyes, and anything in anyone else's eye grossed me out—including contact lenses. I don't know how people do it.

Once I got past her eye, I noticed a dog that was not shy but also wasn't aggressive at all. She was assertive with the other dogs but showed no aggression. Rosie walked around our home like she owned it, and she didn't strut, but her gait reflected confidence. She was also overweight. Based on her disposition and body mass, we assumed that she might have belonged to a senior citizen who overfed her. Perhaps her former owner moved into a facility that did not allow dogs, maybe her owner got sick and could no longer care for her, or maybe her owner had died. The sending shelter had no information on Rosie, so these were all guesses.

For her size and shape (she had short legs and was barrel-chested), Rosie ran and jumped with no problem. You might expect a dog with short, stubby legs to be unable to keep up with dogs who had longer legs and were not overweight. But Rosie ran in the yard and chased them just like any other dog we had. When it came time to sleep, Rosie had no trouble making the jump up onto our bed.

Where Rosie excelled, however, was her molding to your body position wherever you sat. If you were in a chair, Rosie would climb up and sit on your lap. Then she would cuddle up to you and take the shape of your body. Her body matched the contours of your body, like putty or clay. I seriously thought of renaming her *Clay* because she molded to everyone's body. If you were lying on the couch, same thing—just in a more horizontal position. Her reputation grew both in our house and out; friends and family who visited wanted to sit with Rosie and feel her love.

All you had to do was start rubbing her belly, and you could be assured that she was not moving for anything. She was like this with everyone. Elissa tried her best to get Rosie to see her as her favorite. It didn't happen. I tried the same thing, same results. Both Matt and Corey made valiant efforts as well, but all that did was give them aching arms as they ended up petting her for hours with nothing to show for it. It was almost like Rosie was intent on proving to everyone that she was not going to be exclusively loyal to anyone. She had no favorites in our house in the weeks and months that followed. She simply enjoyed the touch of a human next to her. All she asked in return for sharing her love was a gentle stroke of your fingers on her belly.

Rosie's refusal to show favoritism to anyone began to change with the regular visits of the associate pastor from our church. Ginny started coming over to get help from Matt and Elissa on her new blog. She was starting a blog and needed some guidance getting it up and running. Since she was born in the same era as Elissa and I, where we didn't grow up with technology, Matt seemed like the perfect person to help her out. Elissa taught web design and graphic design, so her expertise was also invaluable. I just stood back and made them believe I understood what they were talking about.

Ginny visited with us every Thursday evening after dinner. Everyone in the house began looking forward to our "Thursdays with Ginny," as we affectionately called them (referring to the title from Mitch Album's bestselling book, *Tuesdays with Morrie*). Not only did we humans look forward to the visits, but the four-legged family members got excited. It didn't take long for the dogs to start getting antsy by the front door around seven o'clock every Thursday night. How they knew, we do not know. Maybe it was Elissa getting the water going so Ginny could have her cup of tea when she arrived. Who knows? All we knew is every member of our family—two- and four-legged ones—looked forward to these visits.

Once the blog was up and running, the visits turned to more personal topics where we began to share each other's lives with one another. We shared in confidence, not ever worrying that we might be embarrassed later on. We shared just about everything—our successes, failures, fears, and especially our faith. Ginny gave Elissa and me the strength to question things and move forward in our faith journey. Together we examined scripture and ancient history. We talked about what might be possible and where we might end up. It was both challenging and enlightening as we stretched our minds. We forced them to open up to things we would never have considered if not for Ginny's encouragement and support. Not only did we share desserts, tea, and an occasional dinner, we shared trust in each other's lives.

Of the four dogs now in our home, Rosie was the one who, from the beginning, showed the most interest in Ginny. And guess what? Ginny began showing a preference for Rosie. We would sit in the family or living room, and once seated, Rosie made sure she was the first dog standing in front of Ginny. It wasn't long before Ginny invited Rosie up on the sofa with her, and the rest of the evening was spent talking and laughing, all with Rosie curled up against Ginny. Just like modeling clay.

One Thursday night, Elissa joked with Ginny that since Rosie loved her, Ginny should take her home. Ginny replied that she already had a dog at home, and she was an older dog. Besides, she didn't want the responsibilities of another dog just yet. A week later, after witnessing more of the same love between them, Elissa said that Rosie *looked* like she belonged to Ginny. Since Rosie picked Ginny over anyone else to sit with, and she might as well bite the bullet and get it over with—just adopt her, for Pete's sake! "Nope, not ready yet," was Ginny's response.

As the weeks went on, Ginny's defenses were taking a beating by Rosie's persistence. Now it wasn't enough for Rosie to just sit with Ginny. Rosie began kissing her while cuddling with her. Uh-oh.

Although Ginny never mentioned it, we saw a subtle change in how she talked to Rosie. We found our conversations turning to dog issues and stories. This, mixed with a healthy dose of theology, makes for some interesting banter. I think Ginny knew that she had fallen for Rosie and had to find a way to make her a part of her family.

Now might be a good time to go back a few pages and reread Ginny's blog, the one she wrote the night she took Rosie home. Go ahead.

Did Ginny see something in Rosie? Was she able to see past her eye, past her physical appearance, and see Rosie's heart? Did the ugly duckling realize she was a swan all along?

I think the answers to these questions are, in the order they were asked: Yes. Yes. And yes.

Something magical happens when we allow love in, doesn't it?

We didn't know why Rosie didn't show favoritism to anyone in our home, and it was not as if she was aloof or disinterested. Just the opposite was true of Rosie—she was one of the most loving and affectionate dogs we ever fostered. She loved *everyone!* And she loved the dogs as well. Nothing got her riled. She ignored the cats and played with the dogs when she wanted—on her terms. She acted like the mature one in the pack, like a group of unruly teenagers where one member of that group was thinking smarter than the rest and who was the more mature one, the one who made the right decisions. It's not like this one member didn't want to associate with the others. She enjoyed their company, and she was a loyal friend. This one member just had her act together. She was immediately recognized as the one who established herself as not having to go along with everyone else just because they were her friends. You know that type of person, or teenager, don't you?

We had to wonder if Rosie was simply waiting for the right person to come along. Ginny was getting ready to retire from the ministry. After more than four decades of helping so many people, Ginny was nearing that decision to retire. You should know that she helped countless young people as a school teacher before entering the ministry. She devoted her life to helping others, and now she might be lonely in the years after retirement. If not for Rosie, she might have been very lonely—her Miriam Rose died shortly after she adopted Rosie.

Part of Ginny's hesitation in adopting Rosie was her concern for Miriam Rose, as she did not know if Miriam would accept her. Some years before, Ginny tried to bring another dog into the house, but Miriam Rose rejected that dog, and there were some aggression issues. Ginny would later tell us this wasn't the case with Rosie. Miriam Rose accepted her into the home, and they got along great. Could Miriam Rose have known that she was sick and that Ginny would need someone to fill that void after she was gone? Did Miriam Rose sense something in Rosie that told her she was the one? I would imagine there are skeptics who would argue this was all just one big coincidence—Rosie not attaching herself to anyone in particular until Ginny came into her life; Ginny wanting to adopt a rescue dog that was a large breed with a soft, wavy coat; Miriam becoming sicker as Ginny and Rosie got to know each other better; Ginny deciding when she did to take Rosie home for a trial run; Miriam Rose accepting Rosie into their home; Miriam Rose dying shortly before Ginny decided to retire. All of those things came together in just the proper order for Rosie to be where she is today. It all started with Ginny needing help with an online blog. Einstein said, "There are only two ways to live your life. One is as though nothing is a miracle. The other is as though everything is a miracle."

"Dogs come into our lives to teach us about love, they depart to teach us about love. A new dog never replaces an old dog, it merely expands the heart. If you have loved many dogs, your heart is very big."
—E. Jong

What starts as dark often leads to periods of insight. Sometimes that is how we grow. What could have been the darkest day in Rosie's life turned into the light of ours—the day she arrived in our home. What could have been some of the darkest days in Ginny's life turned into a time of enlightenment. The darkness we all feel inside us from one time or another tends to mask opportunities for growth and understanding; we look at something that makes us feel uncomfortable, and that darkness seeps into our decision-making. We consciously decide to turn away from that which makes us uneasy to make ourselves feel more at ease. It's a nice feeling, and it doesn't take much effort. But the feeling can seem empty.

When I first saw the photo of Rosie that Taryn sent me, I said to myself that her eye didn't look that bad. Then, when I saw it in person, I was shocked. I wanted to turn away. I wanted to *not* deal with it—or her. It was not until I opened myself up to the possibility that she was more than a strange-looking eye (and lower jaw) that I saw her for who she really was. I allowed those dark feelings of uneasiness to blind me from the light of her love. Maybe that was what made Rosie special. Maybe her love (not the mushy, slobbering kind that Eiko showed) lit something inside of everyone who met her. Having experienced it, maybe those people were able to shove that darkness away— the same darkness that I had felt—and opened themselves up to what was possible when they saw Rosie in her true light.

I'm not sure that's what happened with Ginny, though. I do not think she ever felt uneasy around Rosie. I think that is just the way Ginny is. She finds the beauty in what life has to offer, regardless of the outward appearance. And with Rosie, she demonstrated that for me in a way that was both eye-opening and humbling.

When you are a minister, you are supposed to lead by example. My past experience as a kid with an air rifle clouded my vision, both literally and figuratively. It has been said that we are all the sum of our past experiences. Maybe we don't have to be a slave to them, however. Maybe we can learn from them and allow them to serve a purpose for learning more about ourselves and the world around us.

Ginny's love for Rosie served another purpose. It taught us the importance of letting light in, of flipping the switch, that helps us see more clearly. I cannot imagine what it must have been like for Rosie when she was dropped off at that shelter months earlier. We probably all have a picture in our minds of what that could have looked like. While we each have our unique vision of that place, we all probably share a similar feeling about it—it was dark. The atmosphere was dark, the mood was dark, the feelings were dark, and Rosie was facing darkness with each passing day that she wasn't claimed from her concrete and metal wire room.

You and I share in the Good News that is Rosie's life. We share in the joy in Ginny's wisdom of seeing Rosie for who she was and who she was meant to be. It wasn't that long after she adopted Rosie that her Miriam Rose died. It's safe to assume that Rosie arrived in her new home just at the right time. That is the kind of story where they really do *live happily ever after*.

Rosie and Eiko find an unusual item to play tug-of-war:
a pair of the author's underpants!

How can anyone not love Rosie's looks?

8

O Divine Master
BAILEY

I signed up for Aikido lessons after completing a defensive tactics course while a police officer. Aikido seemed to be the right martial art to study as a police officer because I figured I wouldn't need to know how to break a board or do a spinning roundhouse kick if I ever found myself in a bar fight. Most police officers are injured making arrests or subduing unruly people, and the fights they find themselves in are hand-to-hand, close-quarter battles, where *fighting for your life* takes on a very real meaning. A police officer fighting to retain control of his own gun is something that cannot be taken lightly.

Learning wrist locks, pressure points, and throws would serve me better than other self-defense styles. I walked into the dojo for the first time and witnessed men and women dressed in funny robes with different colored belts tied around their waists. The instructor—the sensei—positioned all the newer students at the front of the room while the more experienced students filled the ranks behind. I later learned that this is how things work in the *dojo* (literally translated from Japanese as "Place of the Way"). Newer students are seated (everyone sits *seiza*) during the opening of class, and the place of honor was reserved for new students and students who were not yet advanced in rank. Those students of higher rank sat in order of their ranks, working their way back until the black belt students were in the last row. This idea of new(er) students sitting up front came from traditional Japanese customs where guests sit up front or at the best place at the table. The thought behind this was to make the guest feel welcome and demonstrate that family members, those comfortable in the home, sacrifice their place for another even if that person was a stranger.

The sensei, or teacher, was a master at the art we were there to learn. He was treated with respect and honor, but he didn't act like he was better than anyone. He professed to each of us at every lesson that he was also a student and always would be a student. The founder of Aikido, Morihei Ueshiba, considered himself a student until he died. He said that one never fully masters the art of Aikido. One of his sayings was, "Always a student." It reminded everyone, teachers especially, to remain humble in practicing the martial art he developed.

As I moved up in rank, I learned skills that would serve me well until I retired. As I learned new skills, I developed a sense of pride in the culture and traditions of this martial art that was unknown in this country until the early 1950s. When I was asked to be an instructor of law enforcement officers who would learn special wrist locks, blocks, and throws, as well as handcuffing techniques, my sensei advised me to be careful. He reminded me that I was still a student and would always be a student. That helped me remain humble when the students—from various federal, state, and local law enforcement agencies—referred to me as a master of what we were working on. My sensei's advice, and that of Morihei Ueshiba, rang in my ears and reminded me of the importance of staying humble. No matter how much we think we know, there is always someone who knows more.

"My dog is usually pleased with what I do, because she is not infected with the concept of what I 'should' be doing."
—Lonzo Idolswine

We tend to look up to masters, don't we? We give credence to those who have mastered their craft, and we respect those who are "masterful" at what they do. We set personal goals to master something, be it information for a test, a hobby or skill, maybe even a relationship issue. I know I would like to devote more effort to mastering the art of forgiveness. If you could master one thing in your life, what would it be? Or, put another way, if you knew you would not fail, what is the one thing in life you would like to try?

Elissa and I didn't know if our genius idea of fostering dogs would work out or if we had made a horrible mistake by saying yes. Back then, there was no way of knowing if we had made the right decision. When you first start out on a new journey, there really is no way of knowing if it is smart. You start to discover that after you've taken a few steps in that journey and after you have experienced a few things along the way, only then are you able to start putting things together in your head to come up with a sort of self-assessment of your idea. It can be a scary proposition, can't it?

You have this idea you want to try out, but you are afraid you might fail. You are not sure if it's going to turn out the way you envisioned, and you certainly do not want to look like a fool if the whole thing falls apart or, worse, turns tragic. Aren't these the feelings that stop us from doing something we dreamed of doing? Maybe not entirely these feelings, but they certainly play a role in our decision-making (or lack thereof).

It is probably part of human nature that makes us not want anyone to see our efforts until we've mastered them. That is certainly the way we, in our culture, see our sports heroes. Sports channels don't have highlight reels filled with the hard work put in by these athletes. The reels are filled with unbelievable catches, fantastic goals, and shots scored that didn't look like they had a chance of going in. We see the celebrations with teammates, peers of the hero hoisting them up on their shoulders as if they were the field general who just won the big battle. Sure, there might be a few clips of the hero in their younger years, quick snapshots of what they looked like growing up or in high school or college. But you don't see an hour-long special of nothing but time spent in the gym or on the track, or at the physical therapist's office or with the trainer. That would make for some pretty boring television. We focus on the result—the big play, the grand finale, the winning goal.

I don't think there is one competitor who wants to make the blooper highlights.

You and I join them in going through life not wanting to make the blooper reels, not wanting to be embarrassed or ashamed of what we decided to try. What would our lives *really* look like if we did try that one thing that we knew we could not fail at?

I don't think I'm alone in thinking there is one thing we can try where we do not have to worry about looking foolish. It's called hospitality. When we show hospitality to others, we open more than our front doors—we open our hearts. When we open our hearts without expecting anything in return, we make the *Top 10 Plays of the Day*. It is when we open our hearts and expect something for it that we run the risk of making the blooper reels. Anyone will do something good if they expect a payday from it. Even the most horrible people we can think of will do that. It takes someone who wants to make a difference to open their heart and allow others to benefit instead of themselves.

In his book, *The 3 Promises*, bestselling author and TEDx speaker, David Pollay, talks about the difference between being a guest and being a host—acting like a guest and acting like a host when we're around others. A guest, David says, stays back and watches what goes on. The guest does not start conversations or try to learn more about the others. But a host goes out of their way to make others feel welcome. A host wants to learn more about the guests and wants the guests to feel comfortable and at ease so they can enjoy themselves.

I had not looked at myself as either a guest or a host until I read *The 3 Promises*. But after reading it, I realized that I was a guest a lot of the times in my life. I sat back and watched. Now I guess I could attribute (blame?) that on my years of being a cop. Cops tend not to want to draw attention to themselves in public and always watch others, trying to maintain that tactical advantage that we're taught in the police academy.

Elissa can walk into a room with a bunch of people she has never met, and by the time we're headed home, she knows all their names and a little bit about each one. Me? I'm still trying to remember the name of the host who threw the party. But that is not an excuse to not act like a host or guest and open my heart to learn more about people by making them feel welcome, be it in my home or my journey on planet Earth.

I wonder if dogs feel the same way? After watching all the butt-sniffing that goes on in our house whenever a new foster dog arrives, I think that dogs drop their guard a little quicker and easier than we humans. At least that's the way it has been with Bailey. The little ball of golden fur we brought home from a farm years ago was asked to be a gracious host to every imaginable dog breed, temperament, and personality that we fostered. From Moe and Larry to Eliot and every dog in between, not once did Bailey show anything other than excitement and joy.

Here is the interesting part of her acceptance of other dogs. Because I got sick within a year of bringing Bailey home, we never really socialized her with other dogs. She was never to a dog park, and we rarely (if ever) had someone stop over at our house who had a dog with them. Other than the occasional dog we would pass on our walks, she never had the chance to play with another dog. I hope Bailey forgives me for not getting her out more than we did, and I hope we've made up for it with the opportunities we've given her to be the host.

I could see if she was brought up with other dogs around her how she might be so accepting and gracious. But she was like an only child being asked to share her toys. And her bedroom. And her parents. I'm amazed and thrilled that she made everyone who walked through our door feel welcomed. And what about that word, *welcome?* What does it mean to make someone feel welcome?

How many synonyms can you think of for the word welcome? I'm not talking about thesaurus words (but feel free to use one). I'm asking, when you hear the word *welcome,* what comes to mind? I will bet that if we compared lists right now, we would have an ideal way to treat people!

Bailey didn't need a thesaurus, she didn't need to Google the word to find out how she should act, and she did not need to be told by us how to act. Not once. Somehow she just knew. Was it instinct? Was it an understanding that neither Elissa nor I were aware of? Or was it just the right thing to do because she didn't know any other way to act? She didn't just tolerate all the craziness that ensued. She embraced it. All of it. How many of us would tolerate having our lives turned upside down the way hers was? How many of us would embrace that idea?

When I was still ministering at the church, I would ask the kids what the difference is between tolerating someone and embracing them? This was during one of our Sunday night youth group meetings where the topic of bullying was being discussed. I would ask my teenage charges what it looks like when they tolerate their younger brothers or sisters. Oh, the answers they came up with! That was followed up with listing other things they were asked to tolerate in their young lives. That list included things like their mother's cooking, visiting a family member, having to watch the same television show as their parents, and some of their teachers' quirkiness. When we looked at the list, they were asked if any of the things listed brought feelings of joy or happiness. Without exception, the answer was no. Nothing on the list that they had to tolerate made them happy or brought them joy.

If that's the case, why do schools preach tolerance in anti-bullying campaigns? If you and I are asked to *tolerate* each other, what does that convey? And what does it convey to our children? When used in that context, the word tolerate doesn't have a positive undertone, does it? And yet, we are told we need to tolerate each other in society, to tolerate our differences. When said like that, how can the one doing the tolerating not feel superior to the one being tolerated? Or how does the one *being* tolerated not feel inferior?

In my youth groups, I would ask them to replace the word tolerate with embrace, and then ask them how the other person would feel if they felt embraced instead of being tolerated. I would continue the discussion with the prospect of changing the word tolerate when it comes to our differences with the word embrace. What do their young lives look like? What are the possibilities?

A wise friend of mine, Kevin Touhey, a bestselling author, shared with me a little secret he uses with me. He told me to change out the word expectations with the word possibilities. Instead of expecting a certain number of people to show up at one of my talks, I should think of the possibilities of who might show up. Instead of expecting my youth group to understand a concept I'm trying to present, I should think of the possibilities of what they might learn, and instead of expecting people to act a certain way because of the values I hold, I might want to consider the possibilities of what we might share with each other. In doing that, I welcomed a new way of seeing the world—and myself. Expectations have conditions and can lead to disappointment. Possibilities are endless.

"Man is a dog's idea of what God should be."
—Holbrook Jackson

Did Elissa and I expect Bailey to act a certain way, or did we think about what was possible? I wish I could give a definitive answer one way or the other. I would like to think we considered all the possibilities, but I have to admit that we also had an expectation. I also have to wonder what Bailey thought of us. Here we had changed everything she understood as normal and replaced it with varying forms of chaos. Did she have expectations of us? Or did she just see possibilities in her life?

It has been said dogs live in the moment. They do not understand the concept of worrying about things in the future. What a gift! If Bailey was living in the moment each day we had a foster dog (or dogs) in our home, this girl has a lot to teach everyone. She didn't project her fears of how much heartache these ankle-biters might cause. She didn't concern herself with how much pee or poop (and the occasional puke) would have to be cleaned up the next morning. All she knew was that today mattered. She was not about to trade time from the present for time in the future when she could live her day *today*. How many of us can say that?

In living in the present, she was the master of her domain. She was the queen among all the dogs, each and every one, that stayed in our house. Watching her explain the rules was more than entertaining. It was a lesson in life.

Bailey's first order of business for each new dog was to greet them, and she accomplished this with a wagging tail and ears up and alert. She wasn't about to wait to see if the other dogs liked her before she let them know that they were welcome. She let her body language do the talking by signaling that it was safe inside and she was there to help the newbies have fun.

Next up on her agenda was explaining the rules of the backyard. After the dogs were safely introduced and we were sure they were getting along on their initial walk, they went out back and ran. And ran. And ran some more. They played with toys, but mostly they played with branches and sticks lying about the yard. Bailey gave every dog an escorted tour around the perimeter of the fence and all the good hiding places toward the rear of the property. This was usually done, not through a game of "follow the leader," but instead with a game of "see if you can catch me."

There was a method to our madness, why we allowed the dogs to run and play. It was to tire them out for their baths. Bailey was more than willing to assist us in this endeavor. So as soon as Bailey got them tired out, she led them into the back door for their baths. Only Bailey knew this was coming, and she couldn't wait! You would think a dog might get tired of getting a bath, but not our Bailey. She looked forward to each and every bath. And there was no way she would let us get away with giving another dog a bath without including her. Elissa and I learned (quickly) that our window of time was narrow; it doesn't take that long for young dogs to get their second wind. That's why Elissa prepared the bathroom while they were outside running. Once they came back in, it was all business—the business of bathing. Once again, Bailey was eager to demonstrate for those not accustomed to the ritual of a bath at the Williams' Canine Hotel. She was usually the first one in the shower and the last one out of the shower. As a bonus, for puppies who did not yet know how to shake their wet fur all over the bathroom, Bailey was more than willing to show them. As the two senior canine instructors who oversaw the scent class I was in with Boomer used to say when they saw a Labrador retriever acting like, well, a Labrador retriever, "Labs!"

Dinnertime usually followed the baths, which was the hardest thing for Bailey to teach. She understood that to have her bowl placed in front of her, she had to sit. Until everyone was sitting, no one was getting fed. She would sit right away, but the other dog(s) who were excited to get some vittles in their bellies didn't want to learn any rules at that moment. They wanted to eat. And the longer their bowls of food were held, the more frustrated they got. What Elissa couldn't communicate to the newest pack members, Bailey seemed to have little problem. A few well-placed barks in the direction of the jumping dogs, and they stopped their antics just long enough for Elissa to get their attention back and have them start over. Sure Bailey probably got frustrated at them, but she never acted angrily toward them, and she never snarled if they finished their dinner first and went over and stuck their noses in her bowl.

Playtime in the house was always the next order of business, and Bailey enjoyed showing everyone the ropes inside as much as she did in the backyard. The rules, according to Bailey, were simple. Everyone had to get along. Whether it was an antler or a spot on the sofa, she wanted everyone to get along. The other rule had more to do with decorum than anything else. There was a certain level of rough-housing allowed, but Bailey set that limit, and she was in control of keeping it. If a couple of the puppies began playing too rough, she would run and bark while standing over them until they settled down to a decibel level more to her liking. Again, the barking was more of an attention-getting sound than anything aggressive sounding.

Lastly, Bailey demonstrated how to go to bed. It was simple: Make sure you go to bed with an antler in case you feel like gnawing on something in the middle of the night.

"You don't own a dog, a dog owns you."
—Unknown

Bailey mastered the rules—some of them ours, some hers. In doing so, she also mastered life. She mastered both her life *and* our lives. Dogs look to us humans as their masters; at least that's how it was written up in the plans. That's the way it's supposed to work. In reality, I wonder who is whose master.

I thought Bailey would know who her masters were as soon as we brought her home from that farm as a puppy. It did not take long for all of us—Elissa, Matt, Corey, and me—to understand that she was allowing us to share her house. I imagine that we were not alone in that predicament. I've heard other dog owners talk about their dogs running their homes. Heck, my doctor tells me about his dogs (and cats) ruling his place. He is a well-respected specialist who has patients so loyal to him that we wait hours in order to see him.

Here is what is unique about this doctor: no one complains as they sit there waiting for him because everyone knows what they will get when they get in to see him. This doctor makes you feel like you are the only patient he has when he sees you. He shuts the door behind him, and *he waits.* He waits for you to tell him about yourself and your family, he asks questions about your kids, and what they are up to, then he asks about your goals and hopes. And in between all that, he tells you about his family, kids, and hobbies. And his pets. He always tells you about the latest adventures of his dogs and cats. If you bring a spouse along, the conversation grows to discover how they are doing. If your spouse is Elissa, you find yourself sitting there watching a conversation go on to include every topic under the sun.

For a moment, you forget that you are in an examination room talking to a doctor. For a few minutes, you feel as though you are getting caught up on things with an old friend. It's only after the conversations about you and your goals, and your hopes and fears are over with that you get to talking about how you are feeling. You don't mention your pain or your ailments until you've finished talking about things that are seemingly mundane. After all the benign stuff is done and over with, that's when he gets to work on you. For as long as you are in that room, you are the only thing that matters to him.

That is why his patients wait to see him. We wait for hours and hours in that waiting room. We get to know one another because no one is pissed off that they have to wait. We understand that although he makes his appointments for a certain time, he immediately gets behind schedule as soon as he sees his first patient. The delays snowball through the day until he is hours behind schedule. But that's okay with all of us who wait to see him. This doctor acts the part of a host. He welcomes you and treats you in a way that puts you at ease. His idea of hospitality is that he does not rush things, and he will not be rushed with his patients. He has mastered his trade in a way that doctors from all over refer their patients to him. As a patient, we wait. And we talk about pets, pets that allow us into *their* home.

Bailey doesn't know about time. It has been said that dogs have no concept of time. I would imagine that if she had to wait in a room filled with strangers, she too would make the best of it and act the part of the host. She would want to get to know you, probably by sniffing your crotch. Once you pushed her snout out from between your legs, you would see that she wanted to be your friend. Then you would see her work the room, doing the same thing to everyone sitting there. Bailey would masterfully do her thing until everyone knew a little bit about her. And in doing so, she would be demonstrating hospitality in a way that makes you feel like you are sitting in the front row, in that place of honor.

We humans like to believe that we are the masters of this planet. If that's the case, we need to understand a few things about ourselves and our role as masters. How will we make others feel welcome? Can we see the possibility in others, or will we expect certain things from them? How are we going to show hospitality in a way that is not judgmental?

"Do not neglect to show hospitality to strangers, for by doing that some have entertained angels without knowing it."
(Hebrews 13:2)

We have a responsibility to act the part of what a master needs to be in order to be both successful and compassionate. Our dogs, yours and mine, teach us by example what it means to be a master. They set an example for us not through their actions, but by our response to their actions. They allow us to act the role of master and then evaluate our response to their actions, to their playfulness, to their honest interaction with everyone they meet, and to their love.

If we claim to know a Divine Master, then perhaps we need to act with a sense of humility of heart by allowing others to see how skillfully we've mastered our trades—trades of compassion, hospitality, putting others in the place of honor, and acting the host. Only then can we truly share the Good News of seeing the Divine in what we master.

Bailey always fetched the biggest sticks in the yard.

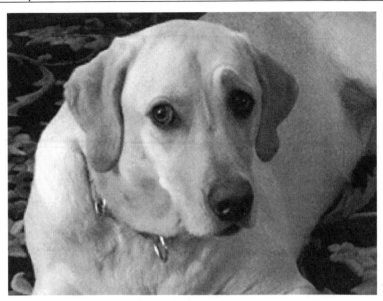

Bailey enjoying a well-deserved rest.

9

***Grant that I may not so much seek to be consoled,
as to console***

BELLA

One of the saddest days in the life of someone who fosters
a dog is when that dog is adopted.

One of the happiest days in the life of someone who
fosters a dog is when that dog is adopted.

Adopting a foster dog is a paradox where an end is a
beginning, saying goodbye means saying hello, and joy brings
tears to the eyes. After a person or family agrees to adopt, the
days that dog is with its foster family pass by with mixed
emotions. Days that once dragged on now seem to fly by in the
blink of an eye. Memories flood your mind from the first day the
dog walked into your home until that moment where you find
yourself gazing at her, recalling all you have been through
together. It was *together*—neither of you got through the days on
your own. You were part of their life, and they were part of your
life. And now, in just a few short days, things are going to be
different for both of you.

You worry about things that you have no control over.
Worrying about them being accepted by their new family, will

they understand all their quirks? You think about all the time you spent together; will they miss me? Your concern includes their emotional wellbeing; will they be happy?

The days tick off the calendar like the days left on your vacation. You find yourself dreading the last couple of days because you know that it's all over once that last day hits. That is the way it feels when you are a foster parent in a rescue organization as soon as you find out one of the dogs in your home is being adopted. It's bittersweet, just like that vacation you enjoyed; you are grateful for the time spent, but you know it cannot last forever. It was never supposed to last forever. It was always going to be a temporary stint to enjoy something special.

There are a few adages out there about the preciousness of time. One of them is, "Make every second count." When the notification comes that one of your foster dogs is going, you realize just how true it is, and you wish you would have appreciated it a lot sooner. We, humans, are a funny species, aren't we? We cannot wait to share all these nice sayings about life, and then it is as if we put them on a shelf until the last minute. You have to wonder what our lives would look like if we really did *make every second count.*

We either wait until we're saying goodbye to a loved one, or we receive life-changing medical news before we see life as both precious and fragile. You would think a guy ordained into the Christian ministry would practice what he preaches. You would think.

Sure I preached it. With almost thirty years in the emergency service field, I have seen my share of death and dying, of pain and suffering. That should be enough to make anyone appreciate every moment, to make every second count. Shouldn't it? As I said, I have preached it to the congregation; I am just a slow learner when it comes to practicing it. It was not until I received my own life-changing diagnosis that I fully grasped the idea that life really is a fragile gift. So allow me to offer some more free advice: Life is short, life is precious, and life is something that should not be taken for granted; make time *now* for what and who you love.

It is times like these that you wish you didn't yell so much, that you had not been so critical of everything; you wish you could take some of the unkind words back. You wish you would have used a different tone of voice. If only you could go back and get a do-over. Oh, how I would make a promise to myself not to say some of the things I *had* said and to make sure I said a lot of things I *had not* said. How about you? Any regrets along the way?

We're in good company, aren't we? I don't think any of this makes us bad people; I think it makes us human. We want to do the right thing, we want to appreciate every minute we are here on this planet, but there are issues that come up along the way. There are issues like the pressures of a job or school, financial obligations, relationship issues, the needs of our family, and if we are lucky, maybe a few hours a week to find a hobby we enjoy. Sure we fail, but it doesn't mean we shouldn't keep trying.

> *"Sometimes the ones who have the brightest smiles have known and endured deep darkness. Knowing this, there is no reason I cannot survive my days with gloomy skies."*
> —Dodinsky

As we appreciate life and realize that we are all human, we also need to acknowledge that we are prone to make mistakes and even make decisions that can harm another. Whether it's due to ignorance or just plain apathy, when we make decisions based on our own best interests instead of those we've been asked to care for, some resolutions need to be made by those in charge.

Without going into details of what transpired, a family that had fostered dogs for our organization for some time was removed from the ranks because a dog in their care was left alone in a home without heat. Due to a powerful storm that hit the area, power outages were widespread, and this family took refuge elsewhere until power could be restored the following day. However, that was one day too long for a dog to be left alone. Even though this dog had food and water and the family returned a couple of times to let it out, it was in the home alone all night long. There really wasn't much of a decision to make about whether or not to keep the family as a foster family with the organization.

We learned about this immediately after the dog was adopted. The action taken was immediate. The dog's name was Bella, and she was a loveable Lab mix—black with a white belly. That belly had black spots all over it. What gave character to her looks was a white stripe that started at the front of her head and ran down her snout, which then widened as it dropped across the right side of her nose. She was as unique as her looks!

The family who adopted Bella had a toddler who was going to enjoy the companionship of his first dog. The love of a dog is so special that I believe every child should have the opportunity to experience it. I know I'm a little biased, but there is even research suggesting owning a pet has positive health benefits. I can still remember the first pet we had growing up. His name was Teddy, and he was a medium-sized dog with white and black fur. My brother and I loved Teddy. But one day, Teddy got loose, and we were never able to find him. I would like to think that someone found Teddy and gave him a loving home. The next dog that came into our home was from our aunt and uncle's farm in Hershey, Pennsylvania. I think our parents felt bad for my brother and me because we had been pining about Teddy for years after he was gone. Our aunt and uncle had a couple of dogs, and one of them, a poodle mix, somehow got herself pregnant.

Our *Fluffy* was born on the farm, and we brought her home as soon as she was weaned from her mother. Fluffy was nothing like Teddy. She was smaller than Teddy, much smaller. The only resemblance she had to a Poodle was her curly hair. Matted hair is probably more accurate. What Fluffy lacked in beauty, she made up for in affection. Fluffy loved everyone, and it was from this dog that my brother and I learned our dog-sitting techniques. That's because both our parents worked, and the responsibility to take care of Fluffy fell on us until they got home. We learned how to walk her, but not how to brush her. Her coat was just too tangled for us to attempt any kind of grooming. That task fell to our mom. Fluffy was with us through our high school years. It was during those years that we learned how to care for a dog.

I still hold those memories dear to my heart, and it is those memories that keep me going when I get upset at things like what happened with the foster family that left Bella alone. Everyone was glad that Bella was going to a family that would give her love and protection and provide comfort to her when a storm came instead of leaving her alone. We all want to find safety when storms hit, don't we? And for those who are scared, comfort is a priority. Bella would not only be given these most basic of needs, but she would also provide them as well.

Bella arrived in her new house with all the fanfare you would expect in a loving home environment. Bella's new parents bought toys and treats as well as personalized food and water bowls. They were excited for her arrival in her new home. A small child waited anxiously at the living room window for his new puppy. You can picture it, can't you?

Bella received all the love she deserved. As a bonus, she had a child to play with. From all accounts, this was a perfect match. A chief concern for any rescue is placing the right dog in the right home. The process to adopt is an intense one, for the main reason that each dog deserves the best home possible. I have to assume that some animal rescue organizations are simply concerned with getting their dogs (and maybe cats, or in the case of our rescue, the occasional potbellied pig) adopted out. It certainly allows for more cash flow. But the reputable ones conduct some kind of background check and home visit before approving any adoption application.

The background check, including veterinary history, personal reference confirmation, and a home visit, were all conducted before Bella's adoption application was approved. And yet, a few days after she was adopted, something went wrong. The family's son, the child who waited by the window for Bella to arrive, was found to be severely allergic to dogs. The family had never had a dog before, so there was no way for them to anticipate this diagnosis. They tried to work it out, but when they had to rush their son to the emergency room because of a severe asthma attack, they knew what they had to do.

We got the call late one afternoon, and Matt and I headed over to the family's home. Their son was at a family member's house when we arrived. He would not be able to come back until Bella was gone and the house thoroughly cleaned. I felt the sadness of the parents as they handed us Bella's food, her leash, a brand new collar that she wasn't quite big enough to fit into, food and water bowls with her name on them, chew toys, and two stuffed animals that she was fond of and kept with her in her crate.

Matt and I tried our best to console them. We wanted to make sure they knew that they did nothing wrong. Finding out about their son's severe reaction now might have been the best thing because they witnessed it while they were home with him. Had they not been home, things could have turned out much worse.

Bella was just as sweet as was reported to us by Taryn, who brought her up to New Jersey in a transport from a shelter in Maryland a few months earlier. The foster family she went to reported that Bella was one of the sweetest dogs they ever had in their home. Once adopted, the family shared with everyone how sweet Bella was. Her photo was plastered all over Facebook as the family wanted to share the joy of their new arrival. Matt and I could see right away why this was such a sad time for the family. Some cynics might be tempted to say that there is no way a family can feel that close to a dog they have had only a couple of days. I would imagine those folks have never had the opportunity to feel the love of a dog. Without any hesitation, Bella followed Matt and me out the front door of the home and jumped in our car. Within fifteen minutes of us pulling up to their house, Bella was on her way to her fourth home in as many months.

"I think dogs are the most amazing creatures; they give us unconditional love. For me they are the role model for being alive."
—Gilda Radner

For all she had been through, Bella was calm and relaxed when she walked into our home. We would have understood if she was a little antsy or maybe even shy. After all, she never had a chance to plant her roots in any one place. What would our lives feel like if we had been moved from place to place the way Bella was? Elissa and I, along with Matt and Corey, thought we would have our hands full trying to socialize Bella as well as make her feel welcome. We felt it was our obligation to her.

We quickly learned that Bella was not only sweet and unbelievably well-adjusted, she was also smart. Bella was so smart that she ended up being the one who taught us about comforting others. As much as we wanted to comfort her, she let us know that she was okay, and she wanted to be the one doing the comforting. She did this by her actions, not her words. She didn't just cuddle when Elissa was stressed about paper grading deadlines or getting her lesson plans done, Bella nudged her hand and laid her chin on Elissa's knee. No words were necessary, and Elissa had no trouble reading what Bella was saying. Bella was telling Elissa to calm down and relax. Elissa did not know how to explain it any better than that; when she was stressed, Bella found her way next to her and made sure Elissa was distracted by petting the side of her neck or stroking the top of her head. It was the same thing with Matt and Corey. She would go over to them when they seemed stressed and do whatever she could to distract them from whatever they were doing that was stressing them out. This was not always the best thing to do as some of Matt's and Corey's stress came from playing video games, and any distraction to killing monsters or enemy bad guys ends in disaster for the player. Apparently, both Matt and Corey had to explain to their teammates why they didn't cover them or why they were not shooting any of the opponents that they said they would. I guess you really do need two hands to play those intense video games.

When Bella saw me sitting in a chair or lying on the couch, she made sure to come over to me and see how I was doing. All the other dogs could be running and playing; Bella would only join them after she checked to see how I was doing. If I was having a bad day, she would stay with me—sometimes she would stay *on* me! It wasn't unusual for Bella to climb up on the couch with me or finagle a way to sit next to me in the chair.

It was not just humans Bella sought to comfort. There were a few days where Bailey wasn't herself, with vomiting and diarrhea. We didn't know what was wrong, but we knew something was going on. Instead of playing with the rest of the pack, Bella stayed with Bailey. She didn't crowd her, but she was obviously concerned and did not want anything to do with the other dogs. Luckily, Bailey recovered without anything more than antibiotics prescribed by Dr. Cobb, who came to our house on her way home from work. Even Dr. Cobb noted Bella's tenderness as she stayed near Bailey while she was examined. One has to wonder if Bella was staying near Bailey out of concern or to keep an eye on Dr. Cobb.

Dwight Moody tells the story of a blind man sitting on a busy street corner holding a lantern. A passerby walked up to him and asked why he had the lantern; after all, he was blind, and the light was of no use to him. The blind man simply replied, "So that others won't stumble and can find their way." Have you ever met a person like the one Dwight Moody described? A person who puts the needs of others before herself?

I don't know about you, but the person I immediately thought of was my mom. She made sure my father, my brother, and I ate the best (usually the *un-burnt*) pieces of food at dinner. My mom was the most compassionate person I know, but cooking meals was not what she was known for. More than once, we would joke that she used the smoke detector as the kitchen timer. In most of her meals, at least one piece of whatever she was cooking was burnt. Each and every time that happened, she made sure that piece of dinner ended up on her plate, not ours. What she lacked in the kitchen, she made up for in love. That meant she would comfort my brother and me before finding comfort for herself. If the house was cold (we did not have much money growing up), she put the afghan she crocheted over my brother or me, not herself. If it was pouring rain and we had to get out of the car, she made sure my brother and I had the umbrella, not her. If bad news hit our family, she would make sure everyone else was okay before she even tried to deal with the incident. When she was diagnosed with breast cancer, her first concern was how my brother and I would handle it, how her need for radiation and chemotherapy would impact *us*, not her.

Bella had that kind of personality, and she made sure everyone, human and canine alike, were comfortable before she could feel at ease. That type of personality is one of a kind. Her actions couldn't be taught, they were instinctive. Some might call it *intuitive*. Whatever it was, it made her special in the eyes of everyone who saw her. There was one lady who saw her picture and read about her on Facebook. This one lady could not help but ask to meet her.

Piglet: "How do you spell love?"

Pooh: "You don't spell it, you feel it."

Author, AA Milne

Sharman is a local school teacher who taught both Matt and Corey. I was fortunate enough to get to know her when I was briefly assigned to the school where she taught. She was a determined and passionate teacher who expected the best from her students. Sharman completed the application, and we set up an appointment for her to come over and meet Bella in person. I knew what was going to happen before she even arrived, but I played along like I wasn't sure if she would like Bella.

I know why I was a little anxious waiting for Sharman to arrive at our home. It's because I always feel like a student whenever I'm around a teacher. I continue to look up to them for what they do and still do not want to disappoint them. I guess that goes back to my childhood, and it was solidified when I witnessed what Elissa went through to prepare for each class. She taught three different courses, and each one needed specific lesson plans. That's three separate lesson plans for each day of the school year. In New Jersey, students go to school 180 days a year.

That's *a lot* of lesson plans! When you also consider the papers that need to be read and the tests that have to be graded, you quickly understand why teachers spend a lot of their off time doing school work. It's enlightening, isn't it? We really do not understand things as well as we think we do until we see them firsthand.

Another reason I still get a little anxious around teachers is because of our relationship throughout the years. Don't get me wrong, I love teachers (and I am *in* love with a teacher). I just have certain memories of being sent to the principal's office. Each and every time it was a teacher who sent me there. My first trip "to the office" was in third grade. What can I say? I wanted to get a head start on everyone else.

By the time I entered high school, my parents were on a first-name basis with each principal I had and a few school board members. I was not officially suspended, however, until the first week of my freshman year of high school. Again, I wanted to get a head start on everyone else. When you do something that evacuates the entire school and gets the fire department dispatched, chances are you are going to get a few days off. In my defense, I was dared to do what I did in an electrical shop class. Luckily, I wasn't shocked or burned. Or killed.

At least now you understand why I was a little anxious awaiting a school teacher to show up at our door. Sharman was greeted at the front door by the entire pack, including Bella. And Bella did not disappoint. She showed Sharman why everyone loved her. Sharman knew right then and there that Bella was going to be hers.

This brings us full circle to the opening of this chapter. Elissa and I, along with Matt and Corey, were thrilled that Bella was getting adopted by someone as caring and compassionate as Sharman. All of us knowing her made it even nicer. The problem would be saying goodbye. As much as we loved seeing our foster dogs get adopted, we hated having to say goodbye. That is true of each and every dog we fostered; this goodbye was as bittersweet as they would come.

This was that paradox, where saying goodbye for one is saying hello for someone else. And certainly, where joy brings tears to the eyes. It was also a time to reflect on all that Bella had taught us.

In this line of the *Prayer of Saint Francis*, the author is asking the Divine Master for strength or guidance or wisdom (maybe all three) that he "May not so much seek to be consoled, as to console." Put another way, instead of seeking to comfort ourselves, we might comfort another instead. Not an easy task when you think about how we humans seek comfort in times of distress. Now it certainly is not hard to comfort another when they are in distress; that is a sign of compassion. But this is suggesting more than just comforting another; this is about comforting another when we ourselves also need comfort, when we're hurting and in need of a compassionate hug or kind word. There is a difference.

When I think of all Bella went through to reach the home of Sharman and her family, I'm dumbfounded by the fact, when considering everything that took place, she sought to comfort more than to be comforted. Bella sought out those in need and tried her best to console them, be they human or canine. Bella could very easily be that blind man sitting on a busy street corner holding a lantern for everyone else. Like the blind man, she was more concerned to see that others wouldn't stumble and to ensure that they found their way.

I imagine you and I can learn a lot from Bella and dogs like her. We have all heard about a dog like this; we've read stories or watched videos on the internet of a fascinating tale of a beloved canine companion. What happens after we close the book or log off our computer? Does the story get absorbed? Do we take the lesson with us? And if we do, how long does it stay? The challenge is not finding stories like Bella's; the challenge is keeping those stories alive in our hearts. We don't need to remember the details. We only have to recall the lesson: Our lives were made better because of those who sought to comfort us instead of finding their comfort. People who made sure we had the piece of food that wasn't burnt, people who made sure we were warm and dry, people who made us feel safe at the risk of their own wellbeing, these are the people we remember.

And now and then, we recall how we were made to feel by watching a pet teach us about life. Sharman and her family renamed Bella *Raven*, and I cannot think of a name better suited for this wonderful creature. According to National Geographic, the raven is an intelligent bird that gathers in flocks during the winter and at night, presumably for protection. They are believed to mate for life, and both parents care for their young. The raven, once almost brought to the point of extinction, can now be found from the icy Artic to the warm Mediterranean, as well as urban areas.

Like her namesake, Bella has adapted to a variety of climates and locales. She has been in places that were icy cold. But she ended up in a home filled with warmth. She was almost brought to the point of extinction, she was bounced from house to house, and she was asked to adjust each time she landed someplace new. But through it all, she never got her feathers ruffled; she maintained an air about her that said she was okay, that she had it all under control. Bella made sure the flock she found herself in was warm and dry, and they felt protected. Every one of them.

Good News does not always travel through conventional means. Sometimes it can be shared through the eyes of a dog.

Bella enjoyed curling up on this chair every day she was with us.

10

To be understood, as to understand

KLAUS

Returning a dog because a child is severely allergic to it, such as in Bella's case, is one of those rare circumstances where a family has no choice. It's heart-wrenching, and it's more of a rational decision than a choice. A rational decision is when you avoid the seafood bar because you are deathly allergic to shellfish; a choice is opting for the Caesar salad over the tossed salad.

A rational decision is based on need, not want. Returning a dog because of genuine health risks is a sensible decision. Returning a dog you bought your child as a Christmas present because it got too big *is not* a sensible decision—it is a choice. These kinds of choices people make with their pets drive people who work with rescues out of their minds.

If you want to see something sad, visit your local shelter anywhere from the end of February through April. This is the time frame when shelters start receiving unwanted Christmas presents, pets that were cute as kittens or puppies on December 25th but lost their cuteness as they became bigger and more destructive. Parents who thought their young children would enjoy that doggie they picked out in early December learned that kids at that age will not take care of a pet no matter how much they promise. All the walks that the twelve-year-old said he would take care of had a lot less priority than his friend's new PlayStation game. "I'll walk him when I get home" became the plea as he was running out the door. All the poop that the adolescent daughter promised to pick up in the yard quickly overwhelmed her, and she lost interest in all but the fun things to do with her new puppy.

The parents found themselves having less and less patience until one day, when they saw that this Christmas gift really was not working out, that it was time to say goodbye. They chose to get rid of something that wasn't working out instead of devoting more time to it, instead of demonstrating to their children that hard work and perseverance pay dividends in the end.

That one day usually arrives two to three months after the gift is given. So anytime between the end of February through April, it is a good bet that you will find returned Christmas presents sitting in cages in shelters across the country. Through no fault of the dog, they end up in a cage instead of a warm family home. They were not part of the decision to be born. They were not part of the decision to be purchased as a gift. They sure as hell did not have any role in the *choice* to get rid of them.

"You must not lose faith in humanity. Humanity is an ocean; if a few drops of the ocean are dirty, the ocean does not become dirty."
—Gandhi

It was a Sunday afternoon when Klaus arrived in our driveway. Klaus was a little more than five months old, and his family brought all of his favorite toys along with him. For as big of a puppy as he was, Klaus was not that sure of himself. We had fostered dogs less than half his size who arrived at our house with more self-confidence than Klaus. His head hung low as his mom explained to us that "He just got too big for our family." She and her husband didn't know he would get that big, and she said it was a really tough decision to let him go. Her daughters were upset by their decision, she told me; however, even though they were in the car that was idling in our driveway, they were never given the opportunity to say goodbye to their Christmas present. Their mom handed me the leash, got in the car, and left. Four little eyes of two precious faces were staring out the back window as their mother drove off.

Just like that, we were the recipients of a returned Christmas gift. Maybe if I had seen the way the girls interacted with Klaus, I would have had a better understanding of why he seemed listless. Maybe he just knew; perhaps he knew his only crime was growing. I would like to think that he had no idea and just thought he was at a new home that would show him the love he deserved.

Even though Klaus was purchased as a Christmas present, he wasn't a full-bred dog. We tend to think puppy mills only deal with full-breeds, but where there is money to be made, well—there is money to be made. Klaus was a mix of three dogs: rottweiler, shepherd, and Labrador retriever. You should have seen the size of his paws! This was a big puppy, and he was going to grow into a big boy.

We had hoped that Bailey would do her thing and bring Klaus out of his shell as she did with all the other dogs we had fostered. While Klaus showed he was a quick study and learned all her rules of the house, he didn't get that gleam in his eyes that would show he was starting to feel at home. He reminded me of our first day with Dakota, and I hoped I wouldn't have to spend another hour on the cold ground out back.

Instead of heading out back in the late winter air, we opted to let it go and observe for a little while. What we witnessed was a room full of dogs bringing Klaus peace offerings, presumably to get him to see they wanted him there. He barely looked any of them in the eye. The other dogs were interested in how he smelled, but he showed no interest in sniffing their butts in return (I can't say I blamed him on that one).

Although Klaus did not seem to be happy in our home, that didn't mean he wasn't hungry. Man, this dog could eat! Watching him eat put a smile on Elissa's face. She gets a special sense of satisfaction when she sees people enjoying her cooking. She gets even happier if you ask for seconds. I tried to make her happy from the first day of our marriage, so I would ask for seconds as often as possible. Do you want to know who this did not make happy? My doctor! Less than a year into our marriage, I discovered I had gained more than ten pounds. The good doc told me to lay off the pasta; Elissa called that advice sacrilege. I am happy to report that I was able to find a happy medium, and the weight is down quite a bit. Would you believe that now my problem is maintaining weight? Sometimes a guy just can't win.

Klaus was eating, so chances were he was not sick. It must be in his head. This should be easy, right? All we needed was a dog psychologist, and we would be in business. Since we didn't have one of those folks handy, we settled for the next best thing: going for a walk. Alone. Whenever we would go on a walk, each of us would take a dog or two. Very rarely did a dog go on a long walk by themselves. After Elissa got the other dogs out the back door, I took Klaus and got his leash hooked to his collar. As soon as I opened the door, he backed up and dug in as I had never seen. He did *not* want to go out that door.

"I used to look at [my dog] Smokey and think, 'If you were a little smarter you could tell me what you were thinking,' and he'd look at me like he was saying, 'If you were a little smarter, I wouldn't have to.'"
—Fred Jungclaus

Okay, now I really needed a canine psychologist. What was going on with him? He ran out the back door with no hesitation. Why was the front door so scary to him? The more I pulled on the leash, the more he pulled in the other direction. I stopped pulling after I saw how upset he was getting. So much for plan B.

Later that night, I noticed that Klaus would not go anywhere near the front door. He would make a wide arc around the entire entryway. If he could avoid it altogether, he would take that route. Instead of walking past the door to go down the hall, he would go in the other direction through the dining room. Klaus wanted no part of the front door for reasons unknown to us. If I wanted to take him on walks of any kind, I guess we would have to leave out the back door.

Except that now he didn't even allow the leash to be attached. There was something negative that he was connecting to whatever we were doing, and whatever we were doing was not working. This went on for days, although it seemed more like weeks or months. One afternoon our next-door neighbor's daughter asked if she could say hi to the dogs. Gabby is a sweet nine-year-old who loved to say hi to the new dogs that arrived at our home. I explained to Gabby how Klaus was a gift from Santa, but he got too big for his home, so his family asked us to take care of him until another family adopted him. Gabby replied that Klaus must have been scared when he got here. I shared with her how scared Klaus looked when he came out of his car in our driveway and how he looked walking into our door to meet everyone. With that, Gabby said, "I bet he doesn't want to go anywhere near that door or your driveway." I could not believe how she could know this. So I asked her, "Gabby, how did you know that?" And that's when she said that he was probably sacred that he was going to be taken to another home where he doesn't know anyone. She continued, "If I were Klaus, I would want to stay right here inside where I knew I was safe. I wouldn't want anyone to take me away."

Out of the mouth of babes.

After almost one full week of trying to figure out what was going on with Klaus, all it took was a small child to see the world the way Klaus saw it. All it took was a small child with an open mind to understand how Klaus must be feeling. All it took was a couple of adults to see the world the way a nine-year-old does. It was a lot cheaper than a doggie psychologist!

Am I the only one who finds wonder in the wisdom of children? When I look back and think of the times I hushed my children when they were trying to tell me something, I'm ashamed not only of how I treated them but also of how many painful things I might have been spared if I had only listened to them. Sometimes, those who think we know the most need to ask for forgiveness the most.

With an understanding of the problem, we could now address it in a way that helped the situation instead of making it worse. One of our dear friends is a dog behavior specialist, and we value her opinion and expertise. One of the things I will never forget Christine telling me is that a dog's life goes by so much faster than ours. What is slow to us is fast to a dog. That's why it is important to have patience with a dog and move slowly as well.

With that in mind, we got to work. The first thing we needed to accomplish was getting Klaus to feel comfortable by the front door. To do this, I attached his leash to him and just let him be. The hardest part of this initial step was convincing the rest of the pack that we were not going for a walk. I don't know what it's like at your house, but when the leashes come out in ours, the pack wants to get moving. We ended up attaching leashes to all the dogs and letting them work out their disappointment on their own. Eventually, they forgot the leashes were attached, and they went about their usual business.

To get Klaus to trust me, I would grab his leash and walk around the kitchen, the room the farthest away from the front door. I would praise him when he walked alongside me and then give him a little treat when he sat. Next up, walking around the house. Slowly. Walking. Around. The house. Each time we got a little closer to the front door. When Klaus acted scared, we would stop and move back a step or two. He let me know where his comfort zone was. And I let him know it was okay, and I wasn't going to push it until he was ready. Every time he calmed down at the edge of the imaginary line that he felt was his comfort zone, he was praised.

It was a two-step-forward, one-step-back process, but eventually, we were able to walk past the front door with very little anxiety on his part. I knew we passed the first hurdle when I let him run around (with the leash attached) and then call him to me. I had positioned myself in the living room, and he had no choice but to walk past the front door to get to me. His reward—another treat.

The next hurdle was to get him to look out the door. To do this, we put all the dogs out back, and I opened the front door, with the full-length glass storm door being the only thing between the inside and the front porch. We called the dogs back inside and let them run around. Klaus never even noticed that the front door was wide open. My goal was to get Klaus to sit at the front door while looking out the storm door. "Slow is fast," I heard in my head. Christine knew what she was talking about. I worked for her for a short period and watched in amazement how she handled dogs that other trainers had given up on. Not only did she have no fear of any dog, but she also had a personality with them that said, "I'm in charge. Everything will be okay, but I'm in charge." When I heard her voice in my head, I knew I had better listen. We worked slowly. I didn't want him to think I was tricking him into something he did not want to do. He was going to do this because he was going to know that it was okay. It took a while, and it was literally two steps forward, one step back. But we eventually made it to the front door and had Klaus sitting there, calm and relaxed as if he did not have a care in the world.

I cannot explain how it happened or exactly when it happened, but during our time together, Klaus and I bonded.

There was a sense of trust—in both directions. Klaus trusted me, and I trusted Klaus. That trust was based on mutual understanding. Klaus needed to understand what I expected of him, and I needed to understand how Klaus saw the world. Once we figured that out together, we had it made. Shortly after Klaus was sitting at the front door (eating training treats that I fed him from my pocket), we were out the front door and in the front yard. Then we were out in the street taking a walk together. And then, we were gone, out of sight from the house and taking in the sights and sounds—and smells—of the neighborhood. We were gone for more than half an hour, and when we returned home, Klaus was welcomed by the rest of the pack, waiting by the door. It was then that I saw the gleam in Klaus's eyes. Klaus was home. Klaus was home safe and sound. And he knew it.

"We have two ears and one mouth so we can listen
twice as much as we speak."
—Epictetus

I've been told, more than once, that I am a slow learner. I have to admit something to all those folks who accused me of that: You were right! But you want to know something? Klaus reminded me that slow is okay. Klaus taught me to slow down and take it easy and that there is no need to rush things. It will all come to you at the right time. How did Klaus teach me this? How did he remind me? It was through the voice of a little girl who wandered over to our house one afternoon when both Elissa and I were at our wits' end trying to figure out what was wrong with Klaus.

Whenever we meet people where they are, on their terms, we are saying to them, "I'm interested in what you have to say." Most of us are familiar with the type of person who dominates a conversation. You know who I'm talking about, don't you? The person(s) you have in mind and the one(s) I have in mind, make sure you know everything about them. They cannot wait to tell you as much as they can. Often as fast as they can. They don't seem very interested in you, do they? They are more interested in you being interested in what they have to say. If you are at a gathering, you watch this person work the room going from group to group, sharing the same things you heard. You are left to wonder if the person really cares about you or your life.

I was fortunate to know a man who was the entertainment editor for a syndicated newspaper. Whenever I saw Lou at gatherings, he came over to me and started a conversation. As soon as he started the conversation, Lou closed his mouth and listened. He maintained eye contact and kept listening. When I was done sharing a thought, Lou asked me to share more about it. He probed deeper to learn more about what I was talking about. He didn't try to figure me out. He just listened with a sense of interest. It was more than just paying attention. It was what some experts call *empathetic listening*. Using empathy while listening to a person share something with you takes practice. It means you put yourself in their shoes as they are talking, as if you are with them and the story being told is being told with you and about you—as if you are the person doing the talking. You don't just see it their way; you experience it the way that person experienced it.

That is what Lou did, not just with me but with everyone he interacted with. He wasn't as interested in you learning about him and his week; instead, he wanted to know about you and what you did that week. Or month. Or last year. Lou did not rush the conversation, and he didn't force the topic. He wanted to understand what you were saying. He wanted to understand you. When you walked away from that conversation, you felt as if your life meant something. You felt as though a person who had interviewed the stars of Hollywood was interested in your life and wanted to be a part of it. That is a gift. Lou enjoyed sharing it.

We all want to be understood. It is one of our needs. Relationships fail because one spouse believes the other *does not understand them*.

"He doesn't understand me."

"She doesn't understand how important this is to me."

"I'll never understand my kids."

"My parents don't understand me."

I would imagine you can add a few of your own to that list. If all of us have a need to be understood, and that's the goal in all of our communication, who is doing the understanding? If folks in a relationship are only worried about being understood instead of understanding, is it any wonder relationships fail at the rate they do? I'm not just talking about partnerships between adults. This disconnect is also between parent and child. You have to wonder if anything is going to change if we do not change the way we go about communicating.

A bad conversation is just a game of waiting for the other person to stop talking so you can talk about what you want that person to hear. But if we make an effort to understand someone on their level, on *their* terms, we have a much better chance to see the world through their eyes. So often, we try to understand a person on our terms; to, in a very twisted way, insist that they see things *our* way so we can understand *them*. It was what Elissa and I were doing with Klaus.

In German, the name Klaus means "victorious people." If we are to have any chance at being victorious in the game of understanding, we first have to see ourselves as our most brutal opponent. It was not until we saw how wrong we were in our approach that we were able to help Klaus become what he was supposed to be—a happy, well-adjusted dog who loves being alive. If we insisted on seeing things through our lens, frustration would have led to anger and resentment. Before you know it, any chance of developing a bond would have been gone.

It took the combined efforts of a little girl and a dog behavior specialist to open my eyes and remind me that by taking my time, both Klaus and I would develop an understanding of each other and what we were struggling with. That understanding led to a desire to learn more. I wanted to learn more about Klaus and what he had to offer the world, and I am sure Klaus wanted to learn more about me so he could trust and just live in the moment. Can you imagine what our lives would look like if we just took a page from what Christine, Klaus, Lou, and Gabby taught me?

- Take your time.
- See it from their perspective.
- Be patient.
- Have a desire to learn about the other person.
- Listen with an empathetic ear.
- Ask follow-up questions.
- Be willing to admit you do not know everything.

Does this list look like a summary of a yearning to understand more than being understood? It has been said that you cannot understand someone while you are talking. Try listening with an empathetic ear next time you have the chance. Be patient with that person who might need a little more time in order to be understood. Don't rush the conversation. Take your time. Make it a point to learn something about the person you did not know before talking. Give it a go. What do you have to lose?

As we move forward in our own journey, we have opportunities to make a difference. Some of us will make a difference in a child's life, others in the life of someone living alone. Maybe we will make a difference in the environment or our workplace. Even more of us will make a difference at our place of worship or a community initiative. There are those who will make a difference in the lives of forgotten animals.

It feels good when we make a difference. It feels even better when we have an understanding of the cause we are working toward. The only way to gain that understanding is to listen in a way that says, "I want to hear you more than I want to be heard." We need to see in a way that shows others we want to see what is in them instead of wanting others to take a look at us. And we need to seek to understand more than we seek to be understood. If we can accomplish this, we might be victorious people in ways we could never have imagined.

This desire to understand is not just Good News for you and me, it is Good News for those in our lives as well.

Klaus took a liking to the same chair Bella loved.

11

To be loved, as to love
ROCKY, PART II

There could be worse things than being called a loser, right? Our skin is not so thin that being called a loser is going to ruin our day, is it? I was a cop for twenty-five years, and I was called all kinds of things, so I was happy when someone remembered to use *all five* fingers when they waved to me! Still, nobody wants to be considered a loser. We all want to be winners.

When you see yourself as being successful in life, you stand a little taller, walk with a little more confidence, and feel good about yourself. You feel like a winner. Everybody loves a winner. If that's all true, then the idea of being loved should come easily to winners. Winners love to be loved. Just watch your favorite team's postgame show. When they win, the fans go nuts and shower the team members with love. But when the team loses— oh, when the team loses. I'm living in and writing this book from the Philadelphia sports market. When one of our teams loses, it's not a pretty sight. Winners catch all the breaks and go far in life. Losers are not expected to go very far, and they get none of the breaks. When you feel like a loser, the only luck you seem to have is bad.

As shared in previous chapters, Elissa and I had dogs come into our homes that other people saw as losers. These owners committed what may be the most unloving act of all in the eyes of a pet: They dropped their pets off at a shelter with no way of knowing what their future would be. However, everyone who surrenders a pet has to know that unless their discarded pet is adopted, they *will* be put to sleep. I cannot think of an act, in the eyes of an animal, that is less loving than that.

When Elissa and I signed on to fostering dogs, we promised ourselves that no matter what, each and every dog that came into our home would feel loved. We knew where these dogs would be coming from, and we knew at least one human in their life felt they were not worth keeping. We couldn't imagine how that must have felt, to be dropped off in a cold, strange place, wondering if you would ever see your owner again. We worried that these dogs might not trust us. Who could blame them? Their last human contact abandoned them; would they be wrong not to trust another human ever again?

We knew there would be a lot of pee and poop, we were advised there would be heartache, and we hoped there would be love. This is a chapter about love, the kind of love you find in the eyes of a dog that has been rescued from a shelter. It is about the love you find in the heart of a dog who was once seen as worthless. This is about the failure of love and the love of failure.

We have had a pack in our home while fostering a variety of the dogs already mentioned. The only dog I mentioned as being ours was Bailey, our yellow Lab. You cannot have a pack of *dog* (singular); you need more than one dog for it to be considered a pack. Where did the other dogs needed to make up a pack come from? We were (and still are) failures! I was told it happens to everyone in rescue programs; sooner or later, everyone in an animal rescue fails. We were no exception.

I need to go back and start at the beginning of where our failures began.

Rocky had been with us for a little more than a month when an application came in on him. We had fostered many dogs before this guy, so we should have expected this day would come. We expected it; we just were not prepared for it.

There was something about this one that melted our hearts, and not in a gooey, mushy way. This melting was the kind that says, "I understand." The message he conveyed was that he was mature enough to understand the craziness that was our home, and he was okay with it. He signaled to Elissa and me something neither one of us could articulate, and yet it was something both of us felt. Independent of each other's thoughts or feelings, the day the application came in, we told one another that we had to talk. You know that feeling when your wife tells you that there is something she needs to talk to you about? That one sentence has led to many a sleepless night for husbands worldwide!

But I had something I needed to share with her as well, so we sat down to talk about what was on our minds. Over a cup of coffee, it was there that we talked about it. Elissa felt it, and I felt it, whatever *it* was. It ended up being the feeling that neither one of us believed: we could not let Rocky go. Both of us had the same feeling at the same time. That's what some call synchronicity. We believed if we both felt the same thing, at the same time, maybe we should listen to whatever the universe was trying to tell us.

We didn't know who the application was from, and we knew nothing about the family that wanted to adopt Rocky. It wasn't like we didn't care. We cared, and part of us felt bad that we were denying a loving home and the chance to experience what Rocky had to offer, especially his love. We also knew that we would offer him love like no one else. We had been doing that all along. Without knowing it as it was happening, we had fallen in love with Rocky. It wasn't until we learned that he would be leaving that we realized just how much we had fallen for him.

We did not have a lot of time to discuss our feelings. Taryn needed to know right away so she could tell the applicant that either Rocky was still available for an appointment to meet him or that he had been adopted. Before Taryn got that last word, "adopted," out of her mouth, I told her that Rocky was not going anywhere. I thought Taryn would be upset by our decision, and I thought we had disappointed her. We were a foster family, and our role was to love them temporarily until they were adopted by a family that would love them forever. Instead of being upset, Taryn laughed and said, "Welcome to the club!" She also shared with me that she had a feeling that we were going to fail with Rocky. She said she heard it in our voices when we spoke on the phone. From the day he arrived until that phone call, Taryn and I talked regularly. Her experience told her that my words conveyed something that she heard in every other foster family who failed: I lost a sense of objectivity. I stopped talking about Rocky with any sense of detachment. Instead, I began talking about him as if he was ours. And here I thought I was doing a pretty good job of hiding my feelings.

"Dogs have a way of finding the people who need them, filling an emptiness we didn't even know we had."
—Thom Jones

It would be nearly impossible to describe the sense of relief we felt after we made this decision. How do you put into words something so deep and so passionate that you barely understand it yourself? It would be like trying to describe the smell of the letter G. Go ahead, see if you can do it. It means something different to everyone, and trying to explain it is worthless. That's how it felt the day Elissa and I decided to adopt Rocky ourselves. It was a mix of emotions that included relief, joy, passion, elation, and love.

Love is that emotion that leads man to do some amazing and crazy things, like adopting a dog that you never intended to adopt when you started. If it's hard to describe our feelings, it was just as hard for everyone who met Rocky. As a foster family, you have to open up your house to others who will come to meet the dogs. When an adoption application is approved, the person (or family) sets up an appointment to visit the dog in your home. It's the first time they will meet the dog they only know from a photo they saw on an internet site.

This is the time in any foster home where you hope your pack is on their best behavior. First impressions are important! More than once, Elissa and I were embarrassed by the antics of one or more of the dogs who were not being considered for adoption but made a point to make their presence known. I cannot say if any of those incidents turned a potential adopter away, but they sure made things interesting.

Without exception, each family that came to our home to meet a dog they had put an application on asked if Rocky was available for adoption. And each friend or family member who visited and met him asked if he was one of the dogs available to be adopted. Elissa and I would constantly joke with anyone who came over that they had to leave with a dog! It was our not-so-subtle way of doing our part to get the dogs adopted. They would decline our offer to take a foster dog home with them, but they said if Rocky were available, they would take him. Everyone felt something when they met him. They might not have been able to articulate it, but they felt *it*. All those comments and inquiries about Rocky only solidified the affirmation we already felt, and we had (and have) no regrets. We know we made the right decision.

One of the first things we needed to do now that he was ours was to make an appointment with Dr. Cobb. The sending shelter advised our organization that Rocky was about ten months old. When Dr. Cobb examined him, she said he was well past ten months old; she could tell by his teeth. There were no puppy teeth left in his mouth, and the teeth he did have were solidly planted and had been there a while—this was evidenced by the amount of tartar that had built up on them.

Here we thought we knew his approximate age, and we were wrong. How wrong were we? How far off was the estimate the sending shelter made? We were off by at least two or three years. That was Dr. Cobb's best guess, and she cautioned us that that was all it was, a best guess. With absolutely no record to go on, we were guessing about many things. But overall, Rocky was in great physical shape, and after a couple of vaccinations, we were out the door and on our way home with our new three-year-old dog. Since we didn't know when his real birthday was, we decided that his new birthday would be the day we adopted him!

We were now a family with two dogs of our own. That meant Bailey now had an assistant for her job in new dog orientation at the Williams' Canine Hotel. But what would Rocky's role be? What was he good at? For all the time he had been with us, we didn't really notice any demonstrative activity that established him as having any certain skill set. As it played out, Rocky's role was to be the voice of reason. He maintained calm. Just by his presence alone, Rocky set a tone that expressed what we as a family needed: a sense of calm. Where Bailey intervened, Rocky stood back and watched.

"Love is not an emotion. Love is a promise."
—The Doctor, *Doctor Who*

Another attribute Rocky had was his ability to forgive. That was much needed after I had screwed up one afternoon while Elissa was out shopping. With her gone, I had a chance to arrange a few things in the garage that were along a bench that ran across the back wall. It's one of the few tasks she still lets me tinker with. Since I was working in the garage, I let the dogs out the rear garage door into a small fenced-in area and kept an eye on them as I tinkered. No more than five minutes went by then I realized there was no more cleaner left to wipe down the top of the workbench. I called them all back inside through the interior garage door and shut the door. Once they were inside the house, I grabbed my jacket and keys and headed out the door to run to the local hardware store. Since I would still be working in the garage when I returned, I left the overhead door open.

I wasn't gone more than fifteen minutes when I returned to the most heart-stopping sight imaginable: Rocky sitting in the middle of the flower bed in the front yard! He was sitting there, in between a few clumps of decorative grass that we planted the year before. I got out of my Jeep and called him over to me. He did not move. I wasn't sure if he was mad at me or frightened. It was not until I started to walk toward him that he ran up to me and jumped all over me as I got down on one knee and asked him, "What are you doing out here?" I wasn't expecting an answer, but it sure would have been nice to know what he had been thinking.

Once I got inside the house, I realized what I had done—or, in this case, not done. I didn't count all the dogs before I left for the store. I forgot to make sure all the dogs came inside when I called them in the garage. In my haste to get what I needed at the hardware store, I assumed that all the dogs were inside the house. How could I have been so careless? I still look back and think of what I would have done to myself if something had happened to Rocky. What if he had run away and never come back like Teddy had when my brother and I were kids? The thought made me sick to my stomach.

If Rocky could talk, I would like to think that he would tell me he forgave me. I like to imagine a dog loves me that much. The truth is I don't know what he would tell me. Maybe he would call me an idiot and hold a grudge. I wouldn't blame him if he did. But he didn't. He either forgave me or didn't think anything else about it after our reunion in the front yard. I had to wonder, *Would I be that gracious?*

Not only did Rocky act as if it was no big deal, but he flourished and grew in the days, weeks, and months that followed. Could it be that he was simply appreciative that I came back for him? Is it possible that dogs don't have a concept of resentment or evil and Rocky couldn't imagine me doing anything that would purposely hurt him or put him in danger? I have to wonder how different our lives would be if we forgave that quickly. What would our relationships be like if we loved that deeply?

A trait of a dog that we hear repeatedly is that they give unconditional love. If nothing else, the way Rocky dealt with me (compared to the way a human might) serves as an example of unconditional love—love without any condition whatsoever. We would all like to be loved that way, wouldn't we? I will bet more than a few of us believe we deserve to be loved like that.

Can you imagine how that would feel? What would it be like to not worry if the person who loves you will never stop loving you, forever? No matter what you do, the person loving you would keep loving you the same way. Forever.

Yeah, I could live with that. And I will go one better; I think that's the way I love, unconditionally. You too? Good for us, right? We love because that's the kind of good people we are.

Are you sure that's the way you love, Rusty?

Who's that?

It's me, your conscience, Rusty. I'm that voice inside your head.

Hey, I don't have to explain anything to you! I'm a good lover. Just ask my wife.

"Elissa, can you come here a minute?"

You and me, we think we got it going on, and we are not going to let some voice inside our heads tell us anything different! Are we?

Well, I won't speak for you, but I will take this opportunity to throw myself on the sword and admit that maybe I do not always love unconditionally. I love unconditionally most of the time, just not all the time.

Since I'm being honest, I should probably admit that I do not love unconditionally most of the time, but I do love unconditionally a lot of the time. It is about as honest as I can be: I want to love unconditionally. I strive to be the kind of person who loves unconditionally.

Maybe we use that term too loosely, and maybe it should be saved for when we can back it up. I tell anyone who will listen that I love my children unconditionally, and I tell everyone that I love my bride unconditionally. The problem is, I'm not so sure I fully comprehend what that means. I know I've preached about the kind of love mentioned many chapters ago, *agape love*. Agape love is the Greek translation of the love the Apostle Paul used when he wrote the verses read at countless weddings, that letter to the folks in Corinth where he talks about what *love is*.

Let me remind you how it goes. Here is the list, the way it is usually read:

Love is patient;

Love is kind;

[Love] does not envy,

[Love] does not boast,

[Love] is not proud,

[Love] does not dishonor others,

[Love] is not self-seeking,

[Love] is not easily angered,

[Love] keeps no record of wrongs.

Love does not delight in evil, but rejoices with the truth,

[Love] always protects,

[Love] always trusts,

[Love] always hopes,

[Love] always perseveres.

Love never fails.

Now that's a list, wouldn't you agree?

I adapted this list from 1 Corinthians 13:4–8. The actual passage reads like this:

> Love is patient; love is kind; love is not envious or boastful or arrogant or rude. It does not insist on its own way; it is not irritable or resentful; it does not rejoice in wrongdoing but rejoices in the truth. It bears all things, believes all things, hopes all things, endures all things. Love never ends. But as for prophecies, they will come to an end; as for tongues, they will cease; as for knowledge, it will come to an end.

When you go back and look at that list of how Paul described love, I think you will agree that it represents, if nothing else, a form of unconditional love. If this list represents the best in unconditional love, how do you think I stack up against it? Let me help you: not very well.

Let's start at the top. Am I patient? Sometimes I am, but not as often as I would like to be. Am I always patient with Elissa? Was I always patient with Matt and Corey when they were growing up? I'm afraid the answer is no.

Am I kind? I like to think I am. Do I act with kindness all the time? Am I kind to a person who is a jerk? Do I answer Elissa kindly when we're arguing? Nope, nope, and . . . no.

We can go right on down the list. Of course, I'm not envious of anyone or anything. I never boast (I am the best at that, by the way), and I wouldn't think of acting with foolish pride. Need I continue?

🐾

I'm not suggesting you hold yourself against this standard like I just did. No one could possibly act that way *all of the time*. But that doesn't mean we shouldn't strive for it. There is no reason not to try to be the most loving person we can be—to give love more than we seek. Did you notice in that list that nowhere is there a reference to how the writer is made to feel about love? Did you notice it was about the other person, the one being loved?

That, my friend, is unconditional love. As long as I'm feeling good and no one ticks me off, I can act that way all day long. But what happens when I feel lousy, or something affects my day that sucks the joy out of it? How likely am I to act in such a way that I could go down that list and check off each quality? Not very likely.

I'm supposed to act that way and have been *called* to act that way. You know, the "answering a calling" thing ministers do? Why can't I get through that list on any given day of the week? Maybe because I'm human. You?

It does you and me no good to beat ourselves up for falling short. The best we can do is keep doing the best we can do and make today better than yesterday. Some people call that growth. Instead of wishing we were something we are not, we can continue putting one foot in front of the other and be grateful that we have an opportunity to make a difference in the life of someone we love. I don't think that list was supposed to be an all-or-nothing proposition.

"The one absolutely unselfish friend that man can have in this selfish world, the one that never deserts him, the one that never proves ungrateful or treacherous, is his dog... He will kiss the hand that has no food to offer; he will lick the wounds and sores that come in encounters with the roughness of the world . . . When all other friends desert, he remains."
— George G. Vest

If there was ever a living creature that exemplified the majority, if not all, of the attributes we look for when we think of unconditional love, the dog is it. The dog doesn't wait to see if it's loved first. It offers you love and then waits. Dogs seem to seek out those who need love instead of seeking out those who will love them. Rocky was (and is) the epitome of this trait.

It was easy to love Rocky, and it was easy to take care of Rocky. He is the easiest of all the dogs we have ever cared for. The ease of it all lent itself to all of us holding a special place in our hearts for Rocky, and this was before we decided to adopt him. That special place was different for each one of us. We all saw a quality in Rocky, and each of us saw something a little different. But everyone in the house saw the connection between Rocky and me. Elissa described him as a *healer*.

Elissa, Matt, and Corey saw a dog who was in tune with me. They witnessed a dog who knew what other people were feeling, especially me. Rocky ran and played with the other dogs if I was having a good day with relatively little pain. But if I was having a bad day, with significant pain, Rocky wouldn't leave my side. That remains the case to this day.

His most endearing behavior occurs when I'm lying down. If I'm having a bad day and need to lie down, Rocky follows me and lies down with me. There could be an all-out tug-of-war going on in the family room with Rocky enjoying the game, but if I get up from the living room and head upstairs, he immediately stops what he is doing and follows me up the stairs, and jumps in bed waiting for me to get in. It's as if there is some invisible connection between us. If I'm okay, he's a regular dog without a care in the world; if I'm not doing okay, nothing else in the world matters to him but me.

That would be special enough—a dog that is so in tune with you that he stays by your side when you are not feeling well. But it is what he does next that gives Elissa reason to call him a healer.

When I lie in bed, Rocky gets himself next to me and positions his head in the area of my body that's hurting. If my lower back is hurting, Rocky's head will be there; if it's my leg, Rocky's head is next to my leg; if it's my foot, you guessed it, Rocky's head is there. Sometimes it's my neck or head, where Rocky's head can be found. As I lie there waiting for the medication to kick in, Rocky begins to gently lick the part of my body that's in pain.

At first, I tried to push him away. I thought it was just a coincidence. But the more it happened, the more I recognized it as Rocky needing to do what he could (in his canine mind) to make me feel better. I am lucky because Rocky's kisses—his licks—are soft and almost dry. My skin is not covered with his slobber when he licks me, and it is almost as dry as the rest of the skin on my body.

Do his kisses magically take away my pain? No, of course not. But what he does give me is a sense of comfort that medication cannot come close to matching. He is so intent on helping me that if I have covers over me when I lie down, he will burrow under them to get to the part of my body that's in pain. The best part of *Rocky therapy* is that there are no side effects, except for an overwhelming feeling of love.

Rocky exhibited the same behavior when we had Shadow and Bear. He sensed they were sick, and he would lie down next to them and lick the sores on their bodies as well as the growths. We would watch him do this for hours on end, and whatever growths he licked were the first ones to fall off each dog. Can you believe that? The growths that Rocky licked were the ones that fell off, and the sores that he licked were the ones that healed first.

What did Rocky know that no one else knew? How does he know when I'm in pain? How does he know *where* the pain is? Instinctual? That's our best and only guess. All we can do is speculate. We will never know the answers to these questions, but what is unquestionable is Rocky's desire to love.

You and I have desires. We have desires to love and be loved. Our hearts seem to swell when we are loved, our hearts beat faster, and blood rushes throughout our bodies. That happens because of how another person makes us feel. When we take responsibility to love another in a way that does not seek anything in return, we find ourselves heading toward unconditional love. When we seek to love more than to be loved, we not only make that person's day a little better, we make our lives a little better as well. You and me, and everyone else, are all connected in a way that makes us interdependent. When we practice the act of loving, we are generating a chain reaction of emotion. That emotion leads to unlimited possibilities.

Think of where you work, where you live, your family, or an organization you are part of. Now imagine one act of love. Maybe it is being patient or kind, trusting or hopeful, and perhaps even protecting. Whatever it is, imagine how the atmosphere around you would change with just that one act. What would it start? What do you have to lose?

Rocky, as a dog, demonstrates the best qualities we look for in a human. He loves more than he wants to be loved; he seeks to perform acts of love more than he seeks acts of love. Elissa and I sought to love him because of who he was, not because of how he made us feel. I'd like to think that he sought us for the same reason.

When we share a love that is not self-seeking, that serves others instead of us, we not only make our day better, we make everyone's day better. Good News becomes great news for those we love as well as the ones who love us, even if we forget them and find them waiting for us in a flower bed.

Rocky lets Eiko take the lead in asking if he,
Reptar, and Dakota can go outside.

Rocky was the easiest (and calmest) dog we fostered; his demeanor
was just one of the reasons we fell in love with him.

12

For it is in giving that we receive
NEIKO

"What's in a name?"

When Shakespeare wrote this line in the late sixteenth century for his tragic heroine in the play *Romeo and Juliet*, do you think there was any way he could have known we would be using this expression more than four hundred years later? One of the most quoted lines plays out countless times every day in our culture, now in the twenty-first century, a century of technology and a global economy. Sometimes the old becomes new, or at least it's recycled in a purposeful way in our lives.

Remember the first dog that I was responsible for myself, the one I had when I was nineteen years old? His name was Niko, and he was a Siberian husky-shepherd mix. I loved Niko, and he was not only the first dog I was responsible for, he was the first dog I worked with, the first I trained to understand simple commands. We spent hours walking in straight lines along the perimeter of our small yard. I had him in a heel, and my intent was twofold: to teach him the *heel* command and to show him where our property line was. After this was established, we worked on *sit*, *stay*, and *down* commands. More hours of work paid dividends as he seemed to enjoy the training sessions, and our bond grew stronger every day we were together.

Remembering those commands would serve me well years later as a cop working a boring mid-watch shift on a summer afternoon. We had a K9 unit working that day, and I was very familiar with the handler and dog. The handler and I were friends, and I frequently helped him train his partner, Blackjack. And by training, I mean getting chewed up . . . again. This particular afternoon, Blackjack's handler needed me for a different reason. Blackjack got loose from him. He had been let out in a local park by a creek and took off chasing some kind of wild animal. His handler, for obvious reasons, wanted to find him before any of the brass had to be notified.

He called me on the radio and calmly asked me to meet with him at an intersection close to the park. Police officers do this all the time; you've seen them—two police cars parked in opposite directions, right alongside each other. They are usually in a parking lot, off to the side. You are not alone in wondering what they are talking about. Most people think they are just wasting time. The truth is that there are many things that cannot go out over the radio because anyone can pick up the transmissions with a scanner. A shift supervisor doesn't think anything of it when one unit asks another unit to meet at a certain location. That's the way the two of us, Blackjack's handler and I, played it off that afternoon.

We had planned to form a two-person perimeter in the direction Blackjack ran off. I took the side streets leading to the park, and his handler went into the park. We were both on foot, calling his name. We were basically—literally—two cops looking for a lost dog in a park. Nothing special about that, right? Everyone in the department knew Blackjack reacted aggressively to the sound of handcuffs clicking, the sound they make when you are ratcheting them open to put on a bad guy's wrist. Most police canines react this way because this is the sound they hear as a suspect is taken into custody. The dog would love nothing more than for the bad guy to resist. I have to admit, it is a sight to behold.

Not only was I calling his name, but I was also ratcheting my handcuffs up over my head in hopes the sound would draw him to me if he were close enough to hear it. Guess what? It worked! I was standing in the middle of the street with my hand over my head, squeezing my handcuffs, so they opened and closed, making that familiar sound that Blackjack knew all too well. We made eye contact about 150 feet from each other. As soon as he saw where the sound of the handcuffs was coming from, it was as if he had a missile lock on me. He started sprinting toward me the way I had seen him sprint toward me several times when I was training with him. Except for those times, I was wearing a *hit sleeve* on my arm, a thick canvas wrap that protects the agitator from having to get his arm sewn up after the training was complete. I realized this minor problem as he closed in on me at full speed.

As far as what I was thinking and feeling at that moment, what was going through my head, I don't think I could give it justice by typing it out here for you to read. All I knew was I was about to be a chew toy for a highly trained police dog. Instinctively, I assume, I went back to that primitive brain that wants to survive and recalled my training with Niko. With Blackjack within striking range of me and still charging at me, I yelled, "Blackjack, no!" Then I screamed a command I had heard his handler use many times, "Blackjack, out!" I repeated this once more and watched him hit the brakes and stand in front of me, looking like he wasn't sure what to do. I think he was bewildered about whether he should chew me apart or listen to me. I'm grateful he went with the latter of the two. Once I had his attention, I commanded Blackjack to *sit* and *stay*. I contacted Blackjack's handler on the radio and asked him, casually, to meet with me on the street where his partner and I were standing (well, I was standing, his partner was sitting). The look on the handler's face when he pulled up was one of disbelief. He was certain that I would have been bitten and he was prepared to take me to the hospital if needed.

I asked his handler why he thought Blackjack listened to me. He replied because I used his name before giving him the commands. I learned that if you want to get a dog's attention, you first say his name. This is how they were taught in canine school, and all of a police dog's commands start with the dog's name. What's in a name? Sometimes your life is riding on the line—especially if you are a canine officer and your partner is your only backup.

"May every sunrise bring you hope.
May every sunset bring you peace."
—Anonymous

Rocky and Eiko, if you recall, arrived together in our house, they were foster dogs from a shelter down south, and that shelter was going to euthanize them the day after we saved them. What a great feeling knowing we did something that saved another life! It does not matter if it's human life or the life of a defenseless animal; if you can make a difference, you make a difference.

Rocky was the easygoing dog, and Eiko was the wired Belgian Malinois/Akita mix who loved getting into trouble. The previous chapter was all about Rocky and how we failed at fostering by adopting him as our own. If adopting Rocky made us failures, keeping Eiko made us victims of failure. Taryn wanted to do something special for me. She wanted to help make a difference in the life of one of the members of the organization. She chose me. Taryn said that ever since she started the rescue, she wanted to donate a dog that would be used as a service animal and make a person's life better.

When I discovered this act of generosity, I changed Eiko's name to Neiko. I simply added an N to the front of it. I changed his name because he reminded me so much of Niko, the first dog I had as a young adult. It was pronounced exactly the same, just spelled a little differently. I thought by changing his name, there would be a stronger bond. Even though it wasn't a sixteenth-century play, Neiko changed his family loyalty and became mine. He became ours. After all, by assisting me, he would be assisting the entire family. I was grateful beyond words, I still am, for this gift that saved us tens of thousands of dollars.

We all have challenges in our lives, and when we look around, someone will be worse off than we are. Maybe it's best to be grateful for what we have instead of focusing on things that cause us pain.

The chronic physical pain that I deal with on a daily basis sometimes translates to me being a real pain in the butt! There are still things I can do and accomplish. And those things are made easier with a service dog named *Neiko* by my side.

"Dogs have given us their absolute all. We are the center of their universe. We are the focus of their love and faith and trust. They serve us in return for scraps. It is without a doubt the best deal man has ever made."
—Roger Caras

Elissa and I worked like mad to try to get Neiko adopted. We put his face all over our Facebook pages. Corey and Matt did the same on their pages. My Facebook friends checked my page regularly to see what antics Neiko had gotten into. I tried to share our journey with the foster dogs on my page, and it helped share the individual personalities of each dog. Neiko had his own personality and made for some great reading—according to everyone who commented on the photos of the damage I shared.

There were days Elissa wanted to strangle him, and there were days he could do no wrong in her eyes. Me laughing at everything he did probably did not help the situation, but he was so smart that I was often left shaking my head in amazement at what he got himself into. Like the time he opened up the bathroom vanity to get the 750-count box of Q-Tips out so he could play with them in the bedroom. Sure, I regretted that I showed him, once, how to open the drawers in the vanity, but just imagine what 750 Q-Tips look like scattered across a bedroom floor. It was something you had to see in reality to fully appreciate. You can imagine my apprehension when Taryn told me that she was donating Neiko to me, to us. Boy, was Elissa going to be surprised when she got home from work, and I told her the news.

Having a smart, easily bored dog can be both exciting and shocking. Now that Neiko was ours, we knew we had to get him trained by an experienced person who knew how to train service dogs. We had to do it for him, and we had to do it for us—for our sanity and the future of our marriage.

After three different local trainers agreed to help but ended up not following through, Elissa and I found ourselves with a dog who was getting smarter and more bored with every passing day. I turned to the internet in hopes of locating a trainer anywhere in the continental United States. I was hoping somewhere along the I-95 corridor, but I would have taken just about anything by that point. I learned that there are many unscrupulous people out there just waiting to take your money. These people prey on folks like me who need a reputable dog trainer to train a dog for them. When purchased from a specialized trainer, fully trained service dogs can go upward of $20,000. Seeing-eye dogs are considerably more.

Elissa and I felt fortunate that we found a trainer in Jupiter, Florida, who specialized in service dog training and had more than forty years' experience training dogs. We made the two-day trip down I-95 with Neiko in the rear seat. We were excited and scared. We wanted Neiko to succeed and be the dog we believed he was meant to be. But we were scared, too. We would have to leave him there for a minimum of one month before seeing him again.

When we arrived in front of a home serving as the business headquarters for Elite K-9 Academy, we knew things had just got real. I tried not to let Neiko see the worry on my face, and I certainly did not want him to pick up on my feeling of sadness that I wouldn't see him for a month. Any worries we might have had were quickly alleviated when we met the owner, Nick, who came outside to sit on his front porch and talk with us. That time also gave him a chance to evaluate Neiko. Nick said if a dog didn't have the right disposition, it wouldn't matter how smart it was. A dog that will be used as a service dog *must* have a gentle disposition.

After talking about our goals and Nick seeing how Neiko responded to simple commands, we went inside his office and got to business. We met his wife, Jeanneane, who sat down with us and explained how the training process would progress. We had to write down our goals, read rules and a memorandum of understanding, and initial both. We were given more information than I thought I would ever be able to absorb into my brain. That information contained basic obedience commands and hand signals. We were expected to know these when we returned in four weeks. Finally, we signed a contract that included our goals and what Nick and his trainers promised to do.

Elissa and I were given a chance to say goodbye to Neiko before Nick put him in his kennel, a specially designed outbuilding in the backyard that houses no more than five dogs at a time. After saying goodbye to Neiko, Nick put him in his kennel and closed the door. Elissa and I could hear him crying from our car. Leaving that house was the hardest thing I could remember doing in a long time.

Did Neiko think we left him? Did he think we abandoned him just like the dogs that had been abandoned at shelters that had come into our lives? We were heartbroken.

Our drive back to our *snowbird* home in Jensen Beach took less than an hour. During that time, all I could think about was how well Neiko behaved on our two-day drive down to Florida from New Jersey. We had to stop over in a motel, and Neiko had been better behaved than I expected. He was like a different dog. All the anxiety of him acting like an idiot when we checked in was for naught as he sat next to me while Elissa completed the registration paperwork for our room. He was so well-behaved that when the duty manager heard he was being transported down to Florida for service dog training, she waived the fifty-dollar pet fee and wished us the best.

I was playing that over and over in my head. Was Neiko trying to tell us that he would be a good boy and we didn't have to take him to a kennel for a month? Now I was having second thoughts and tempted to tell Elissa to turn the car around and go back to Nick's and get him. Our minds can play havoc with our feelings, can't they? Guilt is a really strong emotion.

I didn't feel like eating, not lunch or dinner. Elissa knew I had to eat and made me a bowl of pasta. She was concerned my blood sugar would plummet if I didn't eat something. My cell phone rang while she was cooking dinner. I didn't recognize the number. It was Nick! His voice was cheerful, and he seemed confused when I asked him what was wrong. Nick said he was calling to let me know that Neiko settled down shortly after we left, and he had a friend in the program, his kennel mate, Chase. Chase was a border collie that Nick was training, and he and Neiko hit it off immediately. Nick said he usually didn't allow two dogs to run in the yard at the same time until he was sure they would get along. But when he saw the way these two looked at each other through the wire that separated their cages, he thought he would allow them to play. And boy, did they play. Nick said they ran around so much that they were now exhausted, lying in their kennels. Nick thought I might want to know that Neiko was fine. He said he wanted to call me to alleviate any concern I might be having and to let me know I had made the right decision. Elissa's pasta never tasted better.

"A dog is not a thing. A thing is replaceable. A dog is not.
A thing doesn't have a heart. A dog's heart is bigger than
any 'thing' you can ever own."
—Elizabeth Parker

Nick told me I could call him every night to check up on Neiko. I told him I didn't want to be a pest. He told me he understood what we were going through, and if I didn't call to see how Neiko was doing in the days and weeks ahead, he would be concerned that we didn't care about him. I think we averaged one call every couple of days for the next month. If Nick wasn't available to answer, he would call back as soon as he could.

Finally, the Saturday came when we would get to see Neiko; not just see him, I had to work with him on what he had learned, and the obedience commands we were told to have down pat. I felt like a little kid. I was nervous and excited and . . . and a little scared. This all got very real for me. I knew I was sick, but I never thought I would be so incapacitated by chronic pain as to need a service dog. I guess I got so caught up in the process of finding a trainer that I did not realize the implications. I had an order from my doctor that stated I would benefit from using a service dog and a statement from our veterinarian, Dr. Cobb, that Neiko didn't show any signs of aggression. Nick required these two pieces of signed paperwork before signing the contract to train Neiko. All the paperwork, planning, and worrying—and now it was all real to me. I really was so physically disabled that the cane I was using was not giving me the support I needed. It was to the point that Elissa wouldn't go out unless someone was home with me. A service dog would not only give me more mobility and the freedom that goes with that, but it would also give Elissa freedom, too. A service dog would give back to both of us a little bit of life that had been slowly taken away over the past four years.

We arrived at Nick's house to find trainers waiting for a group of us service dog handlers to show up. Each dog in the kennel had an owner—a handler—coming to work with them.

This is how it would be every Saturday for as long as it took Neiko and me to gel as a team and attain all the goals I listed when we first met. Each handler was assigned a trainer, and I could hardly wait for my turn to go back in the kennel and get Neiko. Everyone out front was milling around, and Elissa was introducing herself to the trainers, handlers, and the handlers' families who came along. When Neiko heard Elissa's voice, he started barking and howling. By the time I got to the kennel, he was going crazy. The trainer assigned to me stood next to me and watched.

Whenever Neiko met someone, he would jump up and put his front paws on their shoulders. He would then proceed to kiss them until he was pushed away. He did this with everyone he met, including Elissa and me. I opened Neiko's kennel door, and he immediately jumped up on me and started licking my face. He had not seen me in a month, and he was as happy to see me as I was to see him. No sooner did he jump on me than the trainer yelled, "Off!" It was a sharp command with a tug on his leash to reinforce it. Neiko looked at him and went into a seated position. The trainer explained that if I wanted to greet Neiko, I would need to get down on my knees and say hi to him calmly. I tried my best, but I was so overcome by emotion that I hugged him around the neck as tight as possible. He got excited, let out a bark, and jumped on me again. And that got him another tug on his leash. Nick walked in and told me that Neiko was now a service dog in training. He was no longer a pet. Neiko had a purpose in life, he had a job to do, and my job was to help him be the best service dog he could be.

It was tough love from Nick, but he was right. I had to put my needs aside and do what was best for Neiko. This was Neiko's life, and he had a right to have his needs met more than mine. Right now, he needed to show me everything he had learned. We walked out to the front yard, where everyone was waiting with their dogs. When Neiko saw Elissa, he lunged at her and began crying. Now I had to correct him, and I was holding the *smart end* of the leash. I gave a tug on the leash and yelled, "Off!" Neiko immediately got off her shoulders and sat. Elissa's eyes filled with tears.

Nick explained to Elissa what he told me, Neiko was now working, and when a service dog is working, he must be 100 percent *on*, which meant no distractions. Neiko was working with me, and we had to learn to gel as a team. Over the next hour, that is exactly what we did. At the end of the training session, Neiko went back into the kennel, but this time he walked right in and laid down. Chase, who also completed his session, went in next to him and laid down. They had a system going, and they were used to it. I did not want to screw it up, so I told Neiko I would see him next week and left.

Nick required all the handlers to spend at least every Saturday working their dog with a trainer. I asked Nick if we could come more often, and he told me we could come as often as we liked. For the next five weeks, at least three times a week, Elissa and I took the one-hour trip to see Neiko. I worked with him, and Elissa worked with him. We worked on everything Nick taught him. We did public access training where we went to the international airport, the mall, restaurants, diners, and everywhere in between. We walked up flights of stairs together and down flights of stairs together. We worked on Neiko bracing for me when I would lose my balance and stand strong next to me when I fell.

Neiko was fitted with a special harness with a rigid handle at the top. I use this for mobility support when we walk and to help pull me up off the ground if I fall. Of all the things we learned, Neiko's favorite was to brace. When he braced, I was able to lay on top of him, completely on top of his shoulders if I needed to. When we were practicing this, Neiko's ears went back, and he leaned into me in a supportive and loving way. He was in his glory, leaning up against me, knowing I was dependent on him for safety.

After more than two months of intense training, Neiko was ready to come home with us. It was conditional on the agreement that we continue to go to Nick's house at least three times a week until he believed Neiko had finished his training. We could not be happier, and not only did Elissa and I look forward to the trip, but Neiko also could not wait to jump in the car, knowing where we were heading. We prepared our snowbird home for our departure. Neiko passed the Canine Good Citizenship test, and we continued our public access work. Neiko ignored anyone and any animal around him. He paid attention to me and me alone when he worked—he loved *going to work*!

At home, Neiko would not (and still does not) leave my side. Although he doesn't lick the painful parts of my body like Rocky, he absolutely knows when I'm in pain, and he sits or lies at my side wherever I go. It is a bond that has gotten stronger every day. The time we spent together was unlike any other time I've spent with a dog.

When I was in canine training with Boomer, we completed four hundred hours of scent work. We had formed a bond that was noticeable by every member of the police department and my family. Boomer was my partner, and we counted on each other to do the job of finding explosive devices. It was a bond that I still feel to this day. I couldn't compare that bond to anything else and wouldn't try to compare the love we had for each other. It would be useless. That was one bond. The bond I feel with Neiko is a different kind of bond. Neiko knows, somehow, that I need him in a way that no other dog can help me. He knows I am dependent on him, he understands the situation, and he loves being a part of my life.

That kind of love is almost unexplainable. It is love based on giving oneself for a cause greater than one's own. When we give unconditionally, we change the way the world was working before that moment in time. We set into motion a chain reaction that transforms reality to what it is—to what it should be. If we didn't act the way we did, everything following that moment of inaction is without our name on it. History, forever, will reflect that we did nothing and things went on in the same direction. If we do act and give from the heart, history will forever be changed because of our desire to make a difference.

Neiko received so much in his training and was now a service dog because he gave so much. Elissa and I received so much in our training with Neiko because we were willing to put so much time and effort into it.

What I received from a dog that we were willing to give up on is, quite simply, a gift. Neiko was a gift to me from Taryn, but I also see that he was sent to me by forces I cannot see or fully understand. He was dumped at a shelter at ten months old. He ended up at our home and almost destroyed it when he was there before he was trained. He came close to being given up on because his foster parents were too lazy to give him the time and energy he needed. It was pure luck that we found Elite K-9 Academy and Nick, who saw the potential in him. He excelled in his training, and he loves his work.

Neiko would not be the dog he is if it were not for the idea of giving. At every step along the way, someone had to give for Neiko to move to the next phase of his life. Someone had to be willing to change history right then and there. Neiko received and continues to receive love, but it was through his giving of himself that he received everything. I received more than I ever could have imagined at a time when I needed it the most. But I first had to be willing to give: I had to be willing to give Neiko a chance, I had to be willing to give the time needed to train him, I had to be willing to give in to the diagnosis and prognosis that made me look at myself and give an honest opinion of what I saw, and I had to be willing to give a damn about life again.

In giving, we really do receive. We receive more than we'll ever fully understand. When we give, we change the course of history by setting a chain reaction in motion that will forever have our name stamped on it. Good News never traveled so fast.

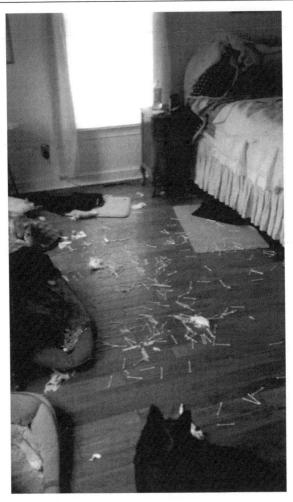

Never teach a Belgian Malinois/Akita mix how to open
the drawers to a bathroom vanity.

The author and Neiko learning to walk together
during their training.

13

It is in pardoning that we are pardoned
BOOTS AND SOCKS

I sent an email one morning to Elissa, who was at her work, to let her know how my day had started. I tried to keep her in the loop before she retired. It kept current the connection she felt with all the foster dogs in the house.

Here it is, the email I sent Elissa on a cold January morning:

> I got up and put the dogs out; all went out except for Neiko – who decided he wanted to stay in bed.
>
> I poured myself a cup of coffee and sat down.
>
> Then Bailey decided she had to go out back, so I got up and put her out.
>
> Next, I refereed the playing in the family room.
>
> Took my first sip of coffee.
>
> Baily barked at the back door, so I got up to let her in.
>
> The *Bailey game* began as she ran away from the door each time I got up to let her in.
>
> I noticed the dog's water bowls were nearly empty, so I filled them.
>
> Took my second sip of coffee.

Bailey finally decided she really wanted to come inside, so in she came.

When I let Bailey in, I noticed Neiko left me a small lake in the kitchen.

Got out the mop and went to town on that mess.

Sat back down for my third sip of coffee.

Watched Bailey puke up everything she had for breakfast (and then some) in the family room.

Now the fun began – everyone thought it was their second feeding of the morning.

Made a valiant effort to stop Boots and Socks from eating Bailey's puke.

Realized my arm isn't long enough to reach from the family room to the kitchen sink to grab the paper towels.

Dragged Neiko into the dining room.

Pushed three dogs away from the puke.

Ran to the kitchen to get the paper towels and the trash can.

Dragged Dakota into the bathroom.

Pushed two dogs away from the puke.

Cleaned up puke with my hands while using my elbows to keep two dogs away from it.

Proud of myself that I was able to multitask like that.

Went to the sink to wash my hands.

Watched Neiko take a massive dump in the kitchen while I was washing my hands.

Cleaned up Neiko's second *gift* of the day.

Took a sip of my coffee – it was ice cold.

Put coffee in microwave.

Sat back down to enjoy my coffee.

Burnt my tongue because the coffee was so friggin hot.

Now watching six dogs sleeping in the family room.

I'm exhausted.

How's your morning going?

This was just one morning of one day that we were fostering dogs. It's not unusual for a foster home to go through this regularly. If a rescue has twenty homes fostering dogs, it can get real messy. Collectively, that rescue organization can be generating a lot of waste on any given day. Not only do foster families have a lot of pee, poop, and puke to clean up, but they have many stories, both funny and heartwarming.

These funny and heartwarming stories were carried into the classroom by Elissa. Every morning she would write three Ps on the board. At the start of each of her classes, the students were asked to guess how many of the Ps Elissa had to clean up that morning before she arrived at school. The three Ps represented *pee*, *poop*, and *puke*. The students who guessed closest to the actual number received a culinary treat.

The stories shared so far are just a sampling of what it was like at our home, affectionately named the Williams' Canine Hotel by a few people on Facebook who were following the antics I posted on my page. Stories of puppies being puppies warm our hearts. We look at what they do with a sense of wonder, and we tend to be more understanding when they get into trouble. We certainly would not allow an adult dog to get away with the things we let puppies get away with.

Puppies chew on your stuff, and you tell them to stop. When your adult dog does it, you punish them like your teenage daughter for not coming home on time. Puppies pee on the floor day after day; it's no big deal. When your grown dog does it once, you lose it. Puppies scratch you with their sharp nails; it is what puppies do. When your older dog does it, you yell at them. Puppies jump all over people when they come over, and you laugh and talk about puppy breath. When your five-year-old Lab does it, she gets yelled at. Puppies sure do get away with a lot, don't they?

Is it because we look at dogs the way we look at children? We give smaller, younger children the benefit of the doubt, but older children should know better. That certainly is true of kids, but what about dogs? Do dogs have the ability to connect the dots and put all the pieces of the puzzle together to understand why they are being corrected? We treat them like they should understand our human words and phrases, but the reality is dogs probably do not understand why they get yelled at so often, why they get their faces shoved in urine and feces, why they get (literally) thrown outside.

The research that I'm familiar with says you have about three seconds to connect a voice cue with an action by the dog. In other words, when a dog does something, you have no more than three seconds to acknowledge it for the dog to understand that what you are saying is connected to what they just did. This works for both positive reinforcement and corrections. If your dog does something that pleases you or completes a task they are learning to do, you have three seconds to praise them for that. That's the positive reinforcement part. Conversely, if your dog does something that is unacceptable, you have three seconds to get their attention and take corrective action.

This means if you come home to a pile of poop on the kitchen floor, rubbing your dog's nose in it does not do anything other than make you look like a bully in your dog's eyes. Imagine if your child was at school and the teacher walked over to her and screamed at her, never told her what she should be doing (the expected behavior), and then walked away in disgust and didn't talk to her the rest of the class period. Would you be upset if your child came home and told you this happened? I bet you would. Especially if your child told you she had no idea why her teacher was so upset. Your child was doing her work like the rest of the class, and the next thing she knew was that the teacher had an outburst and directed it at her. I know I would be at the school the following morning.

This information is based on what I learned while working for Christine, the dog behavioral specialist, Nick, Neiko's trainer, and my ten weeks working with some of the best police canine trainers in the business when I was in explosive detection school with Boomer. I'm not suggesting anyone treat their dog a certain way, nor am I advocating any specific type of training or dog rearing. I strongly recommend you seek professional advice for any type of issue related to your dog.

"There is no psychiatrist in the world like a puppy licking your face."
—Ben Williams

When two little unnamed puppies arrived in our home one Sunday evening, Elissa and I were ready for just about anything.

We had been through our share of dogs, and nothing phased us anymore. Besides, puppies are cute, and we were looking forward to a dose of cuteness in our house. These puppies were saved from a high-kill shelter and were part of a transport of fifteen total dogs that our organization took in on that transport. They looked like Lab mixes and could not be more than twelve weeks old. Their coats were pitch black, and each puppy had white coloring on its paws. The puppy with more white on his paws, the one with the white that went farther up his legs, was named *Boots*. The other puppy, with less white on his paws, was named *Socks*. Their names helped us not only identify them, but also kept them straight in our minds.

At the time they arrived, we had our Bailey, Rocky, and Neiko and were still fostering Dakota. Two puppies should be able to keep this pack on their toes for a while, and maybe if they tired the pack out, Elissa and I would get some rest. It turned out that the last expectation did not pan out.

Boots and Socks had exactly the amount of energy you would expect in three-month-old puppies. They not only tired the pack out, but they also tired us out as well! They were curious about everything. And I mean *everything*. We couldn't turn our backs for a minute without them getting into some kind of trouble. The more I thought about it, the more I thought we must have been nuts this time. The four dogs in our home were well-adjusted, and we were basically on autopilot. There was a routine and everyone, humans and dogs, were on the same page. Now we made a decision that threw a wrench into the process. What were we thinking?

Boots and Socks were not the first puppies we had in the house that discovered the joy of a roll of toilet paper. I guess they saw it as a challenge—a full roll placed in a holder on the wall—to see how far down the hall they could take it without it tearing. If it was a contest, I couldn't say who won. All I saw was the aftermath: toilet paper strewn up and down the hallway, down the stairs, and back up into the bathroom. And every time I discovered the culprit, I would find them standing in the middle of the mess with their tails wagging as if to ask me if I was proud of them.

It would seem that if it takes x amount of energy to clean up after four dogs, the addition of two more dogs should increase that energy requirement by fifty percent. However, when those two additional dogs are puppies, and their names are Boots and Socks, the required amount of energy (and patience) increased exponentially by a factor of eight! This was especially true of cleaning windows and doors—nose prints were also a huge matter.

Our back and front storm doors are full-view glass doors. The living, family, and dining room windows all have low sills. Dogs of any size have no problem looking out. Being the curious puppies they were, Boots and Socks wanted to see everything out the back door, everything out the front door, and everything out every window on the first floor. When two puppies look interested in something going on in the yard, it's only natural that the other dogs want to see what they are missing. The first to join them at the door was usually Dakota; she wanted to make sure everything was safe out there. Next up would be Bailey, who would bounce up and down excited to see anything different.

Rocky would gradually make his way in between the bodies of dogs to ensure a sense of decorum. And of course, Neiko had to push his way in there to take charge of anything that might happen, such as barking. Neiko took the lead in orchestrating that event in the house.

Six sets of nose prints, but not equally distributed, were on every window pane in the house. Our bedroom windows on the second floor gave all the dogs a better vantage point to see the entire front yard and street. Visitations by a flock of geese that lived in a pond down the street was always a cause for celebration for the pack. I think the geese waddled down to our front yard just to see how pissed off they could get every dog in the house.

One particular morning I decided to sleep in. Elissa had already gone to work, and it was just the dogs and me in the house. I woke up groggy and was on my way to the bathroom. Granted, all of my senses were not yet fully functioning, but I recall a peculiar smell. It was right at that time that my brain was connecting with the olfactory system that I stepped in *it*—in my bare feet.

I do not know how to dance, not one step. At wedding receptions, I'm the guy standing at the bar, off to the side, watching everyone's moves on the dance floor. I can't dance one lick. But on that particular morning, I perfected the Cha-cha, the Twist, and the Electric Slide—all without missing a beat!

At least I was near the bathroom, where I was able to grab handfuls of toilet paper and clean the *mess* out from between my toes. And then jump in the tub. Then get back out to clean the tub with bleach. And then get back in to take a shower.

I clean the tub differently than Elissa does. One of the most frightening and upsetting sights I ever witnessed in my life (and remember, I was a cop for twenty-five years and a paramedic for four years before that) was when I walked in on Elissa cleaning the tub one Saturday morning. I walked into the bathroom, and the first thing that hit me was the smell of bleach. In Elissa's mind, if a little bleach is a good thing, a lot of bleach is a better thing. Over the years, our bathtub walls and the glass shower doors have been repeatedly subjected to more bleach than what a crime scene clean-up crew would use.

I had stepped into the bathroom to find Elissa standing in the tub, holding a bottle of spray bleach in one hand a scrub brush in the other, completely naked. *Com-plete-ly* naked. Completely naked except for wearing a pair of yellow dishwashing gloves. There was my bride, standing in the tub, naked, wearing a pair of bright yellow dishwashing gloves, and all she could muster was, "Hey, what's up?"

What's up? My fear level is what was up! I wondered what the hell was going on? Her response was one of indifference. She couldn't understand why I was so upset. She told me this was the way she has always cleaned the tub because this way, she wouldn't ruin her clothes by getting bleach splashed on them. And then she went right back to scrubbing the tub walls.

As I've said, I have seen a lot of sick stuff in my life. But this one . . . this one hit me hard. Some things cannot be unseen.

When there are a half-dozen dogs in your home, two of them puppies, there is usually an odor of bleach somewhere in the house. There is usually something that you wish you had not seen, something that cannot be unseen. That includes things you wish guests in your house did not have to see as well.

> *"The great pleasure of a dog is that you may make a fool of yourself with him and not only will he not scold you, but he will make a fool of himself too."*
> —Samuel Butler

When a prospective adopter makes an appointment, you do everything you can to make a good first impression. If you have a wife like mine, you usually stand out of the way and let her clean the entire house to make it look and smell like you don't have any dogs living in it at all. Even with six dogs living in the house, Elissa did everything she could to make it seem like our house—the interior—looked and smelled like it belonged in a magazine. If it did belong in a magazine, I would have suggested *Mad Magazine*.

It didn't matter how many dogs we had in the Williams' Canine Hotel. Elissa believed the way the house looked was a reflection of the people living there, so she did everything she could to make it look presentable. Floors and furniture were vacuumed, and floors were vacuumed again after the furniture. Air freshener was sprayed, and candles were lit. God, do we have a lot of candles. Not just a candle in every room; we have multiple candles in every room. And not one of them is the same scent. Talk about a synergy of smells. What doesn't smell like bleach in our house smells like potpourri!

We were told there was an approved application for Socks, and they wanted to see him that afternoon. As had become our routine and game plan, Elissa would introduce herself and welcome the people into our home while I contained the rest of the pack outside in the backyard. Then, I would come into the house, introduce myself, and share whatever information on the dog they were interested in. We would answer any questions the people might have and make sure they felt comfortable for their initial meeting with the dog.

After I had the dogs settled out back, I came into the house and met the family that was interested in Socks. It was a mother and her two young daughters. Socks had run upstairs when this family arrived, presumably to bring them a toy to play with. He had a habit of hiding his toys under our bed, and we assumed that was what he was doing while we got to know this mother and her children. They seemed nice enough, just not overly friendly. They didn't laugh at any of my jokes. That should have been an omen.

We called for Socks a few times during our conversation. The girls seemed eager to meet him. Elissa and I wondered what he was doing up there. Here we were, down at the foot of the stairs, and Socks didn't want to make his grand entrance. Finally, after we ran out of things to say, I called for him one last time. And just like that, he appeared. He rounded the corner of the hallway at the top of the stairs.

Picture, if you will, three adults and two children standing at the bottom of a staircase, all of them looking up to the top of the stairs. The landing at the top of the staircase was a blank slate, a clean palette for a lasting picture for a mother and her two small children who wanted to see a creature they were hoping to connect with. Now envision this: a small black puppy appears, carrying a pair of my dirty underwear in his mouth. Socks had gone into the hamper in the bathroom and pulled out a pair of my dirty underwear. Whatever his intentions were, we only knew that we had to find a way to explain this.

Elissa nearly peed herself laughing, I almost crapped my pants, and the two little girls were giggling like mad. On the other hand, their mother did not find this the least bit amusing. If this was not the most ironic, un-choreographed comedic scene in the history of dog fostering, I don't know what would be!

The more we laughed, the more upset this mother became. Thankfully Socks dropped them at the top of the stairs before he trotted down to meet everyone. He jumped up on the girls just like you would expect a puppy to do. The girls squealed and got down on the floor to play with him. I tried to explain how curious Socks was about everything around him. I did this in hopes of explaining away this incident that didn't sit well with the matriarch of this family. I'm pretty sure all the explaining in the world could not change her opinion of Socks. They left about five minutes later, by far the shortest visit we ever had for a dog. We never heard back from them.

Maybe it was for the best that this family had no interest in Socks. I cannot imagine a dog thriving in a home without humor, without people in it laughing—laughing at things that happen in the world and laughing at themselves.

I am happy to share that the next family who visited Socks immediately fell in love with him. Like the first family, they also had two small children. But unlike the first family, this one laughed at Socks' hijinks, and they could laugh at themselves. Elissa had tears in her eyes as she held Socks in her lap on the short fifteen-minute trip to their home a few nights after their visit. This family was inviting, and we stayed with them for about an hour talking and laughing. When we left to head back home, Elissa again had tears in her eyes. But this time, they were tears of joy.

We were down to five dogs now, and before we knew it, an application came in for Boots. This family we knew. Their children were older than the family who had adopted Socks. Both their children went to the high school where I was assigned and Elissa taught. Their oldest daughter knew Matt, and I knew the mother. This family had shown interest in Boots and everything to do with our rescue organization through Facebook comments. Evelyn sent me an email asking about Boots and asked if she and her son, Connor, could stop by.

Evelyn and Connor came over the next day. Connor was still recuperating from a serious illness, and he and I compared notes of where we were in our recovery. They were not visiting to discuss illness recovery; they had come over to meet Boots. Boots did not disappoint. He ran right over to Connor, sitting on the couch, and jumped in his lap. Connor looked over at Evelyn and said, "Mom, look, he already loves me!" That was all I needed to hear.

Evelyn and Connor stayed for about an hour, with Boots hanging around Connor more than anyone else in the house. Evelyn wanted to bring the rest of the family over before giving the final okay. And a few days later, Evelyn and Connor came back with Evelyn's husband, Jason, and Connor's older sister,

Erin. Once again, Boots gravitated toward Connor, but he had no problem making himself known to all the other members of Connor's family as well. Time seemed to fly by as we laughed and shared stories about our families. We found reasons to laugh. This was the family who deserved Boots, and I was sure they would show him love and affection in ways that he deserved as well.

The following evening we were on our way to their home with Boots, who was riding on Elissa's lap just as Socks had done weeks earlier. Our drive was less than half the time it took to drop off Socks because it was around the corner from our home. This time Elissa didn't have time to cry; we were there in less than five minutes. Boots' new family had the house waiting for him. He had everything a growing puppy could want.

Within two weeks, we had said goodbye to two of the most unruly puppies that were ever in our home. Now we had to deal with the realization that instead of being glad they were out of our hair, we were overjoyed that they had adopted families that would love them the way they deserved. Yeah, I said *they* had adopted their families. Sometimes foster dogs adopt their families as often as families adopt foster dogs.

> *"Our dogs will love and admire the meanest of us, and feed
> our colossal vanity with their uncritical homage."*
> —Agnes Repleir

Why were we sad to see two little troublemakers go? Why were we not thrilled to be able to get back to our routine and be able to relax a little bit? Why did we not rejoice that we would finally be able to see out of our windows again? What was it that allowed us to laugh instead of getting mad at them? Over and over again, Boots and Socks gave us reason after reason to get mad at them, and all we could do now, when we looked back, was to laugh. We remembered and smiled as we cleaned those nose prints off our windows and doors.

Wonderful things happen when we let go of garbage and grab hold of gratitude. When we focus on pardoning others for their mistakes, we find our lives become lighter. We are no longer bogged down with all that stuff we've been lugging around. It is as if by forgiving others, we have forgiven ourselves for making life harder than it was supposed to be. Let's face it, when you carry around a grudge, it weighs you down. Everything seems to revolve around the grudge. Comments by others that are completely innocent remind you of the person you resent. Then your thoughts start to play games, and the next thing you know, you are finding more reasons to hold on to that anger you had in the beginning.

When we forgive—pardon—we free ourselves from the burden of balancing the books. It is often only then that we see how much our own lives need pardoning. We become more in tune with those around us, becoming more aware of our words and the tone of our voice. Then we see the need to be forgiven by others.

Boots and Socks could have been remembered as difficult, two puppies that created havoc in our lives and in the lives of the dogs who were already living in our home. If Elissa and I, as well as Matt and Corey and their friends (shoes eaten, jackets peed on, snacks eaten), had not forgiven Boots and Socks for what they had done, our lives would have never been as rich as they had become. We would never have met Socks' family and learned about their children. We would have never been able to learn more about Evelyn and Connor, their family, and their love for Boots, who they renamed *Hendry*. They loved Hendry so much that they even set up an Instagram account and Facebook page for him.

I learned from someone I saw as just a kid until I spent a few hours with him and his mom. Sharing my stories with Connor, some very personal issues, and hearing Connor's experiences helped me learn how to handle a few of the more embarrassing symptoms of my disease. May I be forgiven for not seeing the face of God in this young man all the years that I had known him.

If each year in a dog's life equals about seven of our years, that means with the six dogs we had in our home at the time, we had a house full of toddlers, teenagers, and adults. I'm not sure which is more challenging—trying to figure out how each age group sees the world or how a dog sees the world? One thing is sure, they all have a unique perspective on what is happening just on the other side of their front door. As hard as it is explaining to a couple of puppies what they are looking at, it can be even harder to explain to a toddler, a teenager, and frequently, an adult.

Maybe every once in a while, the best thing we can do is share in their sense of wonder. Instead of figuring out what they are seeing, or trying to explain it all to them, maybe they just need to know that we are there with them – that we forgive them and our pardon is unconditional.

Maybe all they need is to know that we're looking out the door with them and wondering. In doing so, perhaps the mess they make—the nose prints they leave on the glass—will not seem like such a problem in our world. Like footprints in the sand, they leave a story behind.

Dirty underwear, ripped-up toilet paper, and nose prints can be reminders of our need to be forgiven more than anyone else we know. Funny, isn't it? Good News sometimes hides where we least expect to find it. Do not ever accuse God of not having a sense of humor.

I was going to get out the Windex and grab a paper towel to start cleaning the nose prints off the front storm door. Instead, I think I'll leave them for a while.

Boots looks like he's wearing
white boots on his paws.

The learning curve where puppies figure out
cats rule can be an interesting one.

Yep, they did that to our bedroom.

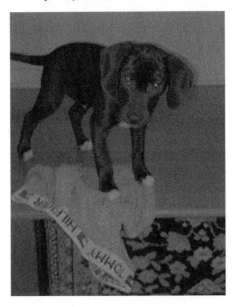

Socks with the author's underwear
during an important meet and greet.

14

And it is in dying that we are born to eternal life
YOU AND ME

This chapter *is not* about death and dying. At least not in the physical sense, or clinically, as defined as the loss of pulse and spontaneous respiration.

The idea of dying is scary, though, isn't it? For most people, the thought of dying is scarier than the idea of death itself. Dying is a process; death is final. Do you see what the author of the *Prayer of Saint Francis* wrote in the next to the last line (the title of this chapter)? The author used the word dying, not death. Dying is present tense; death is past tense. Why do you think the author of this prayer used the present tense form of the word?

I don't understand why the line doesn't read, "And it is in *death* that we are born into Eternal Life." But when you read it that way and compare it to how it's written and has been said for almost one hundred years, you can see a definite contrast in meanings. Let's stick with the way it was written for the rest of this chapter.

This idea of dying is scary. The topic makes people feel uncomfortable. What if we can work our way past the fear of the topic and see it in a way that, while still uncomfortable, won't make us want to run away from the topic?

"So many conditions of happiness are available—
more than enough for you to be happy right now.
You don't have to run into the future in order to get more."
—Thich Nhat Hanh

We cannot get to someplace else if we are not willing to leave where we are in the first place. You cannot get there if you are not willing to leave here. It is a process to get *there*, wherever and whatever *there* is to you. If *there* is a place you want to be once you learn and grow from life's events, you have to be willing to let go of the old you. In essence, you have to be willing to let the old you (or part of the old you) die. In the dying of the old you, you are remade into the person you want to be. You've arrived at that place you had in mind when you decided to learn and grow. It's how we've all grown, how we've all gotten to this point in our lives. It is also how shelter dogs become foster dogs who become adopted dogs. It is the process of how a house is transformed, over and over again, into a home.

The idea of everlasting life, if not a scary thought, is undoubtedly a topic of strong opinions. But what if this is not referring to a perpetual life in whatever form of paradise we envision? What if, for the matter of this book, everlasting life meant something different from our idea of salvation? Our names can live on forever. The memory of our lives can, and should, go on for time eternal. They should be, in that context, everlasting. But it is not up to others to make that happen, as if they are responsible for maintaining a collection of news clippings and photos of our time here on earth. That responsibility falls to you and me.

Our legacy, the history of our lives, is written by us; you and me, we are the authors of our legacy. What we do during our time here is how we're going to be remembered. The differences we make today in the life of another will affect future generations. We might be gone physically, but the impact of what we accomplished will remain undying. Mark Twain had words of wisdom when he said, "Twenty years from now you will be more disappointed by the things you didn't do than by the ones you did."

Our legacy is the total of everything accomplished in life, and I'm not talking about job titles, wealth, or possessions. Our accomplishments must include how we helped others and how we made a difference in the life of someone who was in need. If not, it is just history. History refers to the past, to antiquity. Legacy refers to something handed down from the past; it has a deeper and more personal meaning.

From the first to the last, the dogs that came into our home taught everyone who came in contact with them something about the idea of a legacy. Each one of them was reborn. Again and again, they were reborn into a new life, from the first families that had them to their time in a shelter. And then from the shelter to our home. Finally, from our home to their *fur-ever* home (as it's called in the animal rescue world). Their past died for each new beginning to take place. Their past died each time they grew. Each time they moved from one place to the next, they left their past behind. When they arrived at their new home, they started over again. Even though it took a little time for some, they did it with tails wagging.

Situations that were unknown to them became familiar, and they adjusted. And then they flourished. They left their mark on every heart they touched—from the shelter to our home to their new homes where they now run and play with owners who will love them forever. The legacy of each dog is being etched in time; day by day and minute by minute, they are creating their legacy by making life just a little better for everyone they meet.

You and I can do it, too. Sure our tails will not be wagging, but we can go through life with a smile on our faces. We can show love instead of hate, and we can forgive and instill faith in those whose lives seem uncertain. We can offer hope by brightening someone's day. And we can do it all with a sense of joy that is contagious. We can seek out those who need comfort and understanding, and we can seek to love those who need it the most. We can give in a way that never seemed possible before, and we can allow ourselves to be forgiven. We really can do all these things, and it's not like any of them are going to cost us anything. But we first have to be willing to be used as an instrument. And we need to be willing to die.

Once we understand the idea of what it truly means to be used as an instrument, to be a part of something greater than ourselves, our lives are opened up in incredible ways. Remember, it's not the physical dying that we are talking about here; it is allowing the part of you that was holding you back to die off. In allowing that dying process to occur, we allow ourselves to learn and to grow.

Had Elissa and I not been willing to let go of what we knew to be stable and secure, like a house that was not turned upside down, we never would have learned all the lessons we experienced by getting involved with a cause that was greater than our own needs. We would never have grown into the people we are right now. That part of our lives, before we were crazy enough to say yes to this fun, is still there as part of our history. We cannot erase the past. But the selfish parts of us that didn't want dog hair all over the house, the self-seeking behaviors we had that gave security to the status quo, and the egos that made us believe it was all about us and our survival (even in the midst of a life-changing rare illness) have all died. It was a process, and it did not happen overnight.

Like the physical process of dying, changing our hearts was a process that took time. At times, it was painful, and it felt like we were suffering. We didn't give up, and it's not because we never had that thought in our heads. There was more than one time when either one of us told the other to call Taryn and tell her to come over and get a dog (or dogs) that was causing so much chaos that we felt like it was just too much.

Have you ever been there? Ever felt like it was just too much? You are in good company again! My journey has been anything but easy. My family's lives have been changed dramatically without their consent; a wife who was married a little more than a year had her life turned upside down, and two children who were being taken care of by their father had to learn how to take care of him.

I am right there with you some days when I feel like it's just too much. Life is not necessarily fair, and there are times when I wish I could throw in the towel. Whenever I feel like that, I think of those who are counting on me and those whom I count on. Two legs or four, there is a legacy to write, a story that needs to be etched every second of every day.

What do you want your legacy to look like? What eternal word will be said about you? That word (or words) was never meant to be silenced. It just takes a spark, and before we know it, we are making a difference in the life of someone who needs help. A smile to a stranger, a compliment to a coworker, holding the door for someone who needs some extra time getting from one place to another, forgiving a loved one, asking your child for forgiveness, hugging your partner, and saying those three words: I love you.

It is not going to be one big thing or a great project that makes that chain reaction get going. It will be a little thing, something small, the first domino to fall. Small things are done with big hearts; that's what is going to change things.

"When the world is so complicated, the simple gift of friendship is within all of our hands."
—Maria Shriver

As an ordained minister, I get called to do a fair share of funerals. They remind me of a poem that has become one of my favorites, titled, *The Dash*. Linda Ellis wrote it shortly after her grandmother's death. In it, Ms. Ellis talks about the importance of "living our dash," the dash that is etched on our tombstones between our date of birth and the year of our death. I would suggest that we could do more than live our dash; we can turn that dash into an exclamation mark and really make a difference!

Whether a dash or an exclamation mark, it is the time we have here that matters most. The time we are here is a time for living—the new self and the dying of the old self. In between, there is learning and growth, and there are opportunities and successes. There is even pee and poop, heartache, and unconditional love.

Many of us are afraid we will be remembered for our last worst action. We judge ourselves by our own worst actions. Our legacy, the everlasting part of our lives, does not have to be one of fear and judgment. We have all we need right now to make sure we write our legacy: It's our hearts. Our hearts allow us to go through periods of rebirth; like the trees that lose their leaves in the fall and regain them in the spring, like the caterpillar that goes into a cocoon to become a butterfly, and like the tide that falls in the morning and rises in the afternoon. We are remade repeatedly because our hearts keep on beating as the change happens. And when we think with our hearts, beautiful things happen. *Forever* kinds of things happen.

Perhaps you and I are like foster dogs, and we just have not realized it yet. There are times we find ourselves feeling like we've been discarded at some dark, cold place. It could be that we feel like we're on a highway for hours and hours, seemingly going nowhere. Perhaps we are in a new situation where the surroundings are unfamiliar and we don't know a single person, or we might have just landed somewhere where everyone seems to love us.

When we find ourselves thinking we've been dropped off at a shelter with the other discarded misfits of life, it might do us good to remember that it is temporary. No, you are not going to be euthanized. People are scrambling to get a van down there, or an airplane warmed up, so you have a chance in life. There are people that you have never met, right now, plotting to bring you to safety. Even if it is a temporary foster home, you will fit right in and thrive there until you find your forever place—the legacy that you will write.

If you don't feel like you're a shelter dog right now, go out and find one! Seek out a shelter and help someone who feels like they've been discarded like a bag of trash. So many people are hurting and could really use your help. Maybe it's an elderly neighbor, or a friend you haven't spoken to in a while. Go visit your neighbor, call a friend. Your neighbor and your friend deserve better than to believe no one cares.

Just be careful. Like fostering dogs, it can become addictive. And before you know it, you find yourself doing it over and over again, making small differences in a big way.

Does anyone think the song, *What a Wonderful World*, could have been made famous by anyone other than Louis Armstrong? Did you just catch yourself singing the lyrics in your head? Me, too!

What did Louis Armstrong see that we don't see? What did he hear that we do not hear? What stops us from thinking that this really is a wonderful world? I don't know about you, but I do not want my legacy to be a cynical guy who only thought about himself. The legacy that I want to leave is how I live my life *today*. The thought of our legacy is not about a future history book that has yet to be written, our legacy should be written today by us. It *needs* to be written by us today. And every day.

Perhaps in the days and weeks ahead, we can think about how we are etching that exclamation mark, the time we are here on this earth. And we can use that time to consider what we need to let go of, what we need to let die so that we might get to that place where we belong. In doing so, we're not just making history, we are becoming the author of our legacy.

The last bit of Good News in this book you are holding is a reminder that we were made to be born, not just once, but over and over and over again. We experience a rebirth countless times in our lives. Sometimes there is pee and poop, and even heartache in that process, but it always leads to love. Unconditional love.

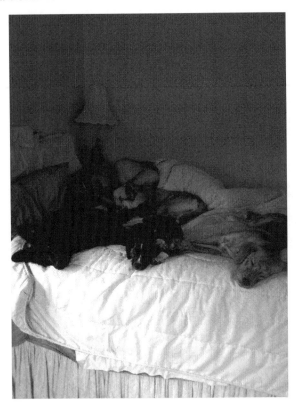

The author finds a place in bed to lay his head.

The author's wife, Elissa, is smothered with puppy love.

Elissa's napping companions include (clockwise from the bottom)
Bailey, Dakota, Neiko, and Rocky.

15

Amen

The author, Bob Perks, tells the story about heartache and love, about life itself.

It's an encounter he witnessed of a man saying goodbye to his daughter in an airport terminal. Bob sees an emotional goodbye and hears each of them say to the other, "I wish you enough."

When the daughter went through the security checkpoint to her gate, her father was left watching her walk away. Bob saw that this man was upset and asked him if he was alright. The older man replied that he just said goodbye to his daughter for the last time. When asked why it was the last time, the man told Bob that he's old and his daughter lives far away. He continued that he had challenges ahead and the next trip back for his daughter would be for his funeral. Bob asked the meaning of them saying to each other, "I wish you enough."

The man replied that that wish had been handed down from other generations; his parents used to tell it everyone. He continued, "When we said, 'I wish you enough.' We were wanting the other person to have a life filled with just enough good things to sustain them." He then shared the following with Bob:

> I wish you enough sun to keep your attitude bright.
>
> I wish you enough rain to appreciate the sun more.
>
> I wish you enough happiness to keep your spirit alive.
>
> I wish you enough pain so that the smallest joys in life appear much bigger.
>
> I wish you enough gain to satisfy your wanting.
>
> I wish you loss to appreciate all that you possess.
>
> I wish you enough "Hello's" to get you through the final "Goodbye."
>
> (Used with permission, Bob Perks, "I Wish You Enough" ©2001)

I would imagine most of us are familiar with the word *Amen*.

When said, out loud or to oneself, at the end of a prayer, it usually means a conclusion by affirmation of what is said. It is like saying, "I approve of everything that has just been shared." Or, in the case of most prayers, what has been asked for. May I humbly ask that you join me in striving for more love and less hate, more pardon and less injury, more faith and less doubt, more hope and less despair, more light and less darkness, more joy and less sadness? Will you join me in seeking to console others more than seeking to be consoled, to understand others more than seeking to be understood, to love others more than seeking to be loved? And to realize how much we receive when we give, and how much we are pardoned when we pardon others?

When we see the world through the eyes of a dog, even a dog that has been discarded and given a death sentence— *especially* through the eyes of a dog that has been discarded and given a death sentence—we begin to understand things in a way that not only opens our eyes, but that opens our hearts as well. Nothing shared in any of the pages of this book has asked or even suggested that you open your wallet to do anything special. This idea of making a difference in the life of another costs us nothing out of our pockets. And yet, it has the potential to make us feel richer than we ever dreamed possible.

An affirmation of any request or incentive can be powerful. It reminds us of the power we have, that *potential energy* that is inside each one of us, energy just waiting to be used. It's the kind of energy in a puppy's tail before it starts to wag. It's stored up and ready to go, and once it gets going, it is very difficult to stop. And it is powerful! If you have ever been hit by the wagging tail of a Labrador retriever, you know the force that's in that tail. And if you are a guy like me who has been hit by that tail, in that area of a guy's body that's very sensitive, you know *exactly* what I'm talking about!

Power can be like that, can't it? It can be used in ways that cause joy and in ways that cause pain. When we affirm or strongly agree with one another that we want to share joy, that we seek to be a force of love, our lives are enhanced by simply helping another. By now, it should be apparent that by thinking of others more than ourselves, we are helped in ways we might not have previously considered. Our lives are enhanced simply by enhancing the life of someone else.

Father James Keller is quoted saying, "A candle loses nothing by lighting another candle." His Holiness, the Dalai Lama, reportedly wrote, "Our prime purpose in life is to help others, and if you can't help them, at least don't hurt them." A guiding principle for physicians, *Primum Non-Nocere*, Latin for "First do no harm," is a revered statement dating back to the nineteenth century (although it is commonly misconstrued to be part of the Hippocratic Oath). Take a look at them. They are phrases from various times in history and from very different social and religious foundations that share a common theme.

They served as declarations for those who heard them. And they continue to be just as important today; you might even say they are eternally relevant, that the legacy of each statement is perpetual.

Simple phrases can do that, can't they? They can last forever in the memories of those who hear them. Things we never remember saying are stored in the hearts of people we know and love, and even in some, we might not ever get the chance to meet.

So, thank you. Thank you for spending some of your time with me. I know how precious time can be, and I truly appreciate that you took the time to share a little bit of my world with me. I wish you the best.

And, *I wish you enough*.

It's time to go now. I have to put the dogs out.

Neiko, Rocky, and Bailey wish you enough.

Acknowledgments

This book would not have been possible without the support, encouragement, and help —real, honest to goodness help—of so many people.

First and foremost, I need to express my gratitude to the members and supporters of Joe Joe's Place Animal Rescue. You are the energy that started all that is written in the pages here. All the foster families in this organization that save dogs in ways few can understand, deserve the accolades. You have all experienced so much pee, poop, and heartache, but also, thankfully, unconditional love. To all of you who have volunteered and sacrificed so much, to those who have given so much of your time, thank you does not seem strong enough. Every one of you needs to know that your work and your labors are your legacies.

Thank you to those who work with dogs every day, the trainers and dog behavioral specialists who devote so much time and energy helping dogs become all they are meant to be. I need to recognize Christine Nolan, dog behavior specialist and creator of Your Dog and You. Christine, your words and wisdom are always at the forefront of my thoughts and actions when working with dogs. Thank you for sharing your insights with my family and me.

Nick Kutsukos, owner of Elite K9 Academy, you didn't just teach me about dogs, you taught me about life. Your knowledge in training service dogs is amazing. You and your staff pushed Elissa and me in ways we never imagined; we owe a debt of gratitude to every trainer on your team. You and your wife, Jeanneane, cared for Neiko with love, and for that, we are grateful. And speaking of love, thank you for telling me to "go write a book." And to Jeanneane, thank you for sharing your time and talents in the early stages of this book, but most importantly, thank you for your friendship, a gift that Elissa and I will always treasure.

Dr. Lori Cobb, Pathways to Wellness Veterinary Care, your devotion to your profession goes well beyond what you've been called to do. And I firmly believe you have answered a calling, an extraordinary calling that very few would even consider. If they could talk, I am certain Rocky and Neiko (as well as Bosco, Boomer, Bailey, Bojangles, and Bellagio) would ask me to convey their gratitude to you and your team for taking care of them, and Elissa and me, all these years.

The members of the Spinal Cord Tumor Association, a community of caring spinal cord tumor survivors, their families, and caregivers, your encouragement and support have helped my family and me in ways that make words seem inadequate. You have not only helped my family cope with the daily struggles of this disease, but you have also given us hope. My prayers are with every one of you.

To those couple of thousand or so friends on social media, some of you I've known most of my life, others for just a few years, and still more I've not had the pleasure of meeting yet in person, you are my cyber friends around the world. None of you fully understand the impact you have had through your comments and posts. I want you to know how much they have encouraged me. You have given me a chance to share my life, and for that, I say thank you.

To my friends, family, and colleagues who have been there for my family and me; to try to name each one of you would be nearly impossible, and I would probably forget someone. Know that you are not nameless, you are precious. You are a precious gift to us, and you know who you are. If you are reading this and we've had a conversation, or you've been to our home, or we've been to your home, or maybe we've met for a cup of coffee, whatever and wherever it was, you made a difference in my life and the life of my family. Know that your legacy includes a cherished friendship.

To my brother and sister-in-law, Glenn and Nancy, and their family, you remind me every day of the importance of family, and without your love and support, neither this book nor my success in life would have been possible. You have been there for us when we needed you the most; you have been there when I was down, and each time you have helped me up – sometimes quite literally. My gratitude goes well beyond what words could convey. I hope I have held up my end of the bargain by giving you all a laugh or two to help ease the pressures of life.

To my children, Matt and Corey, a father never really knows if he is doing it right. But if the result of any test can be measured by its success, then I think I have reason to smile. You two have given me more than just a reason to smile, and you have also given me a purpose in life. I have watched you grow into young men who have taken on a role that you could have never anticipated. You are responsible for this book being what it is. Without you two, I would have never found my passion and my voice to write down what was in my heart. My heart swells with pride whenever I talk about you. Thank you for allowing me to be your father.

To my beautiful bride, Elissa, my soulmate, my lover, my best friend, and my caregiver, what a journey so far! I have managed to write nearly 80,000 words in this book in hopes of conveying a message, so how is it that you leave me speechless? Maybe it's because it would take nearly 80,000 more words to accurately describe my love and gratitude to you. Since that's not possible, I hope I can capture those feelings and write them here.

Through all the craziness that has caused so many ups and downs, you have been the one constant throughout. You have been my rock, and you are my angel. Elissa, this book was your idea; it was your brainchild. You convinced me that what I had to say was worth sharing. The title was born from your thoughts. You were the first proofreader; sitting with me as I typed chapter after chapter, you read them over and corrected my mistakes You were the first editor; you helped me see what I was writing, and you made it better. You were the first to read this book, and it was the smile on your face when you finished the last page that told me we had created something beautiful. The fact is, you are the first one I think of when I open my eyes each morning and the last I think of when I close my eyes at night. Without you, there is no book. From the bottom of my heart, and with all my love, thank you.

Finally, to my mom and dad, I hope I have made you proud. It has been more than thirty years since I've heard your voices or have felt your touch. It has been more than three decades since I smelled your perfume, mom; it has been just as long since I noticed your aftershave, dad. That is a long time to miss someone. I still miss you both every day. What I wouldn't give to hear your voices just one more time; what I wouldn't give to feel your touch, to be able to laugh with you again. Even for just a split second, what I wouldn't give to see you both, just one more time. You, mom, taught me what compassion and empathy looked like. Dad, you shared your sense of humor in such a way that made me want to be just like you. And while I cannot share this joy with you in person, I want everyone to know that you two are as responsible as anyone for this book being written, maybe more than anyone. I know I gave you both a fair share of pee, poop, and heartache. But look at how it ended. It ended with unconditional love. And for that, I am forever grateful.

Other Books By The Author

Tender Truths:
Caring For The Dying
(contributing author)

The Living Eulogy Journal:
A Year of Sharing Gratitude and Becoming Happier

Doubt On Trial:
An Agnositc Minister's Case For Questioning The Bible

Can I Get There From Here:
One Cop's Irreverent Look at Faith

Made in the USA
Middletown, DE
25 November 2022

15991024R00149